Lost and Found

Recovering Our Values,
Reclaiming Our Dream

Rob Baggett

Heart Springs Publishing
Columbia, South Carolina

Heart Springs Publishing, 9 Box Turtle Court, Columbia, SC 29229
(803) 419-2020

Cover design by K. T. Altman

Library of Congress Cataloging in Publication Data

Baggett, Jr., Robert A., 1951-
    Lost and Found: Recovering Our Values, Reclaiming Our
    Dreams/Robert A. Baggett, Jr.
       p.   cm.
       Includes bibliographical references.
       ISBN: 0-9667866-2-9
       1. Values. 2. Character education. 3. Ethics.
       4. Democracy. 5. Education. 6. Parenting. 7. Marriage.
       8. Theology. 9. Family systems theory.

       Library of Congress Control Number: 2003105949

Lost and Found is available at quantity discounts with bulk purchase
for educational, business, or sales promotional use. For information,
please write to: Rob Baggett, P. O. Box 450, Blythewood, SC
29016.

Printed in the United States of America
First Edition

For my wife Teresa, who is still helping me find the answers,
and
for my children, Bryan and Emily – may their generation choose
values that will lead to the fulfillment of democracy's promise.

Acknowledgements

I was fortunate to have been raised by parents who cared about good character. Robert A. Baggett, Sr. and Billie Porter Baggett knew that to be "high class," as my mother once put it, had nothing to do with money and everything to do with how one behaved. Without their kind, firm attention, I would have – no doubt – had a very different life guided by very different values. Along the way, I benefited from the wisdom of a great many other caring people as well. Teachers and leaders at church and school, college and seminary professors, pastors and friends have all played a part in shaping my life and thoughts. Since my marriage in 1980, my in-laws, George and Sue Nesmith and Jerry and Bonnie Knox, have encouraged me and nurtured my dreams. Most of these significant influences are not credited directly in this book, but I owe them a debt all the same.

I would also like to thank several people who generously gave of their time and talents to read my manuscript and make suggestions: Mary Mauriello, Kitty Laing, Rachel Corvi, Carolyn Murphy, Pat G., Annette Burke, Brad Smith, Denise Barth, Brenda Kneece, and especially my wife, Teresa, who always understands what I am trying to say.

Encouragement and much needed guidance on publishing were supplied by Mick Carnett, Nancy Smith and Kris Militello. I could not have done it without them.

Much of *Lost and Found* is structured around the character traits known as the Six Pillars of Character, which were so named by Michael Josephson of the Josephson Institute of Ethics. I am a graduate of the Character Development Seminar sponsored by the Institute and want to do everything that I can to promote these ethical values. Nevertheless, I want to make it clear that the views expressed in this book are mine and mine alone. They are not intended to represent the opinions of Michael Josephson, CHARACTER COUNTS! or of any other person or organization named herein.

Rob Baggett

Table of Contents

Part Three

On Parenting

"Every civilization is only twenty years away from barbarism. For twenty years is all we have to accomplish the task of civilizing the infants... who know nothing of our language, our culture, our religion, our values, or our customs of interpersonal relations."
- Alberta Siegal, Stanford University

Lost and Found

Recovering Our Values,
Reclaiming Our Dream

Introduction

For about thirty years, it was politically incorrect to talk about values. Most academics and many in the media promoted moral relativism, the belief that all values are specific to a particular culture and therefore, relative. "That's a value judgement," they would say to silence those who would promote certain behaviors as the right way to act. Americans were encouraged to be "values free" and to make no judgements about right, wrong or even, better behaviors because "there are no absolutes." Ironically, by taking this position, these activists made *tolerance* an absolute value, automatically eliminating more fundamental ethical values like respect and responsibility. Up was down, and right was wrong. The only bad people were the ones with strong convictions. With constant pressure to conform to the "no-rules" ethic, most adults, including politicians and educators, gave up on transmitting a consistent system of ethical values to children. Young people were expected to figure it out for themselves or, at best, to meet adult expectations that were equivocal and often contradictory. Without any kind of cultural roadmap, too many in our nation got lost.

Now we are in the process of rebuilding our common culture and relearning the language of good character. In the public school where I am employed as a guidance counselor, it is not only OK to talk about values and character, it is mandated. The school and workplace violence that has become an ordinary occurrence in America has forced parents and teachers to face reality: there are limits to individual freedom and children must be taught how to live in harmony with other humans according to traditional norms. They are not going to "pick it up on the streets" and certainly will not learn it from watching television or listening to popular music.

But character education still makes people nervous. Conservatives hope for a return to the days when America was a "Christian" nation dominated by the Judeo-Christian ethic. They propose such things as posting the Ten Commandments in schools and "school choice," which would provide vouchers to help pay for private schools where direct religious instruction is part of the curriculum. Besides, they remember a number of ill-conceived social experiments, such as the values clarification programs of the 1970s. These classes taught, as one student put it, "There is no right or wrong, just good or bad arguments." Liberals and religious minority groups, on the other hand, worry that any type of character education is a way to impose traditional Protestant morality on everyone. It will be the "tyranny of the majority," they cry. Conservatives counter, "Without any standards, we are suffering under the tyranny of the minority. Is that any better?"

Both groups have their points, but we can no longer afford to debate this issue while our society drifts toward chaos. We have a responsibility to communicate clear, consistent ethical values to our children now. Fortunately, a number of very intelligent people who know and care about young people have been working to find an answer to the question, "Whose values are we going to teach?" And at least one of these individuals has developed a program with the kind of depth and authority worthy of the American people.

CHARACTER COUNTS!

Michael Josephson is a lawyer who retired from teaching legal ethics to form the Josephson Institute of Ethics. In 1992, he gathered a diverse group of leaders from youth-serving organizations, both secular and religious, to come up with a set of consensus ethical values we could teach our children. It took them three days to agree, but ultimately, they chose six: trustworthiness, respect, responsibility, fairness, caring and citizenship. The group named these the Six Pillars of Character and issued a declaration, which asserts that these values "transcend cultural, religious and socioeconomic differences." With a common language for teaching ethical values, Mr. Josephson went on to develop the CHARACTER COUNTS! Program, which provides parents, teachers and community leaders with a well-thought-out framework for character education. More than anything else, it gets us past the "Whose values?" question and allows us to declare a truce in the culture war in order to care for our children.

A Matter of Urgency

Because democracy is, as Michael Josephson points out, an ethical movement, it is imperative that we transmit democratic values to our citizens. Universal values such as the Six Pillars of Character are imbedded in our Declaration of Independence and Constitution. By stating them explicitly, we breathe new life into the American ideal of equal freedom, dignity and worth for all people. But unfortunately, many have neglected the duty to impart these values for a generation by pretending to be values free and have even passed laws to encourage people to think of themselves as powerless victims – a most undemocratic mindset. This kind of thinking has been particularly destructive in the public schools where it has become advantageous to be labeled as having a disability or disorder of some kind. In fact, some children have gained "beyond equal" freedom through certain provisions of the Individuals with Disabilities in Education Act (IDEA). It is very difficult to teach character to these children because they cannot be disciplined in the same way as other students. For example, a child with dyslexia, who has trouble telling a 'b' from a 'd,' is treated as though he cannot tell right from wrong. Regardless of what he says or does in school, he is guaranteed a "free, appropriate, public education in the least restrictive environment." For an offense that would automatically put a regular education student up for ex-pulsion, this child would first be entitled to a manifestation hearing to determine whether the child's disability kept him from behaving properly. In most cases, school districts, wanting to avoid the expense of a lawsuit, will decide that the child was unable, rather than unwilling, to obey the rules. Then, strangely, this out of control child is usually returned to his same classroom, leaving his teacher and classmates to wonder what happened to their rights.

The unhappy fact of life in American schools today is that educators like the aforementioned teacher have few rights, but many new responsibilities. When chronically disruptive students are returned to the classroom, they often come with a list of accommodations and other added duties for the teacher. Some of these, such as "preferential seating," also affect other children. For example, if the returning student is easily distracted, he might be seated by one of the best-behaved students, who will be expected to help keep him on task. Decisions like this punish good behavior and reward bad. Is it any wonder that so many of our citizens are ethically illiterate and have developed what might be called an "anti-democratic" character?

Exacerbating our situation is the high number of students who come to school with inadequate family support. In 1960, 1 out of every 20 children born in the United States was born to an unmarried woman. Today, almost 1 out of every 3 is born out of wedlock. This statistic alone may explain many of the discipline problems in our schools. Studies – and experience – show that children raised without fathers often have little respect for authority of any kind. School is sometimes their best hope of receiving the kind of caring discipline they so desperately need. However, the worse a student behaves, the more likely it is that his parent will know his "rights" and will do everything possible to prevent the student from experiencing negative consequences for bad behavior.

It is no coincidence that school violence is on the rise at a time when school officials are facing legal challenges to their attempts to limit bad behavior. According to David Wilmes of the Johnson Institute of Minneapolis, research shows that wherever adults set limits, children will invariably push three to five steps beyond the limits. So, to have a safe school environment, it is essential for parents and teachers to set fairly strict limits. But in the current climate, where bullies are sometimes seen as victims and many parents have learned how to put administrators and teachers on the defensive, the enforcement of reasonably strict rules is an uphill battle.

In the area of violence, the public schools are a reflection of a society where too much disrespectful behavior is tolerated as free speech or as just the expression of a person's culture. This tolerant attitude, more than anything else, is responsible for the increase in disrespect for the equal rights of others, including the right to life itself. The recent series of deadly shootings in our public schools follows a trend that has been going on for quite some time. "During the past two decades nearly half a million Americans have been murdered, and an additional 2.5 million have been wounded by gunfire – more casualties than the U.S. military has suffered in all the wars of the past 200 years," reports Eric Schlosser in the September, 1997 issue of the *Atlantic Monthly*.

With this level of social disintegration, it is not surprising that so many of our law-abiding citizens have retreated into gated communities, private schools and private clubs. This defensive posture was explained to me in a conversation I had with a "pillar" of my community a few years ago. Insisting that public school was not an option for his children, he said, "I believe that America lost its way a long time ago, and my whole strategy is to insulate, insulate, insulate." I am haunted by his comment because I believe he spoke for many of our best citizens and that their withdrawal from public life is proving Edmund Burke's adage: "The only thing necessary for evil to triumph is that good men do nothing." Without the leadership of these morally upright men and women, it will be much more difficult to reverse our democracy's downward spiral.

Mission Possible

If it is true that democracy is an ethical movement, then we have to admit that America has seldom lived up to its own ideals. After all, we have been a work in progress from our beginning as a rebellious British colony, saddled with the institution of slavery. But the drumbeat of freedom has continued through the years and we are now at a point where all the laws are in place to make the American dream a reality for everyone. However, the lack of meaning and connection in our public and private lives is taking its toll. Without a "virtuous citizenry," the dream is becoming, instead, a nightmare.

Before we can reclaim the promise of America, we must address the problem of ethical illiteracy. Philosophers understand that unlimited freedom and complete equality are mutually exclusive goals, but the general public has not given the matter much thought. In fact, most of us act as if we believe that values are a private concern and should never be examined publicly. But the reality is that we live in a nation of many races and cultures, founded on the ideals of equality and freedom, and every important decision we make is based on a value judgement. In other words, it's *all* about values in a democracy.

In the pages of this book, I have attempted to present my best thoughts on the common culture and character necessary to any well-functioning democracy. The first section is made up of longer essays designed to address these issues in some depth and to share what I have learned from reading, listening to and living with other people who have struggled to live ethically. Much of what I have written is not particularly original and could be subtitled "Variations on a Theme by Michael Josephson." This is not surprising since one of my hopes is to promote the Six Pillars of Character as the common language in our continuous conversation on American values. The second section consists of short articles originally written for my school's newsletter, which were designed either to communicate big thoughts in a small space on a sixth grade reading level for the students or to spark the thoughts of parents and teachers who care about character as well as academics.

On the face of it, the task of reeducating Americans in the values of freedom after so many destructive years is a daunting one. Sometimes it seems as though I am teaching ethics as a second language. Even so, my own experience at Blythewood Middle School proves that everyone of us can make a difference and that it is not too late. I have found that universal ethical values like the Six Pillars of Character provide a shared vocabulary for all people of goodwill. These values do indeed transcend cultural boundaries, give meaning to our lives and allow us to reclaim our dreams as a progressive, united people.

What Do You Worship?

"To do good things in the world, first you must know
who you are and what gives meaning in your life."
- Paula P. Brownlee

I once knew a lady who was unusual because she did *not* feel guilty about keeping a less than perfect house. She explained her philosophy simply, saying, "You can make a sin out of housework." What she meant by this, she explained, was that if a parent were too concerned about having an absolutely clean house, her children would not be allowed to feel at home. Sure, they could go out to play in the snow. They would just have to understand that they could never come back in. That would make too much of a mess. In her own way, this mother was doing some clear thinking about values and the way one value competes with another.

Our values are the things we most highly prize and greatly desire. These are the things that motivate us to get up and go into work each day or to lie in bed until noon. It is all a matter of priorities. And so, it is of great importance that we think carefully about what is most valuable to us. Are our relationships with family and friends dearest to our hearts? Or are material things like having the latest electronic gizmo more important? Do we crave financial security? Romance? Adventure? High social status? Freedom? James Fowler of Harvard once wrote that the values of consumerism dominate American life. These values tell us that "you should experience everything you desire, own everything that you want and relate intimately with whomever you wish." In a similar vein, Joseph Campbell, the great interpreter of mythology, commented that the most consistent American value was money.

Their observations bring to mind Jesus' statement: "You cannot serve God and Mammon." Because Mammon, or money, can buy any material thing that you could desire, it is often given a higher place in our lives than the less tangible, but ultimately more lasting ethical values, such as love and respect. But when we give non-ethical values our highest priority, we ensure that we will not achieve the state of happiness we aspire to. Because non-ethical values such as money, social status, and pleasure are extrinsic, they can never give us the satisfaction and inner peace that comes from the intrinsic ethical values that produce a good character and lay the groundwork for personal fulfillment and strong relationships.

This is not to say that non-ethical values are unimportant. They usually relate to our most basic needs. Consider the five needs of humans identified by psychiatrist William Glasser. They are: a need for love and belonging, a need for things necessary to survival, a need for some freedom, a need for some degree of power and a need for fun. Notice that none of these needs are associated with strictly ethical values. We can survive by stealing or by working. We can use our freedom for good or ill. Power corrupts, if we are not very careful. Not all fun is good or clean. Real love is ethical by definition, but what passes for love is often quite manipulative and wrong. And as gangs, cults and bad marriages demonstrate, belonging is too often the product of habit and misplaced loyalty.

For those of us who desire the best that life has to offer, ethical values must come first. The purpose of ethics is to define the *summum bonum* or highest good of life and to define the values necessary for achieving this goal. When we make these values the foundation of our lives, everything else tends to fall into its proper place and some of our other goals are modified. But when we make a non-ethical value an absolute, we eliminate the possibility of ethical living entirely.

One of the best examples of misplaced values in modern life is the way some of us have promoted sex as the ultimate value. You would have to go back to Biblical times and study an ancient fertility cult, complete with temple prostitutes, to find anything to match it. Increasingly, this preoccupation is taking over our lives and communities with no end in sight. To get an idea of what the future of your community could look like, it might be instructive to look at the place in America where the worship of sex has been officially embraced – Las Vegas, Nevada.

⚖

On a trip to the Grand Canyon a few years ago, my family and I got an unintended education in Nevada's community values when we swapped for a timeshare in Las Vegas. This was not a place I particularly wanted to visit; but after reading about how "kid friendly" Las Vegas had become, we convinced ourselves it would be OK. It wasn't. Everywhere we walked, we were assaulted with pictures of all-but-nude women, some of which were blatant advertisements for "Hot Babes Sent to Your Room." It took us awhile to accept that this really was a state where prostitution had been legitimized. To get to any of the so-called "kid friendly" entertainment, you had to walk through miles of casinos and pass numerous ads for things my children didn't need to see. Once there, we were usually disappointed. Only Lance Burton's magic act proved worth the effort. But then, I hadn't *really* expected much from a city founded on gambling and entertainment. When money and pleasure are your highest values, this is what you get.

The ethical climate of the state of Nevada was summed up for me in an article on page 8A of the April 2nd, 1997 edition of the *Las Vegas Sun*. It began "A San Francisco prostitute and sex industry advocate criticized Nevada for excessively regulating its brothels, charging that it forces some women into illegal prostitution." Her chief complaint, aired at a seminar on the politics of the *sex industry* held at the University of Nevada at Las Vegas, was that it was unreasonable to ask poor prostitutes to pay for the state's mandatory testing for HIV, the virus which causes the fatal disease, AIDS. In a culture where sexual freedom is consistently held to be unlimited, even the "consumer's" right to life is considered a lesser value. And so, the quest to extend the boundaries of sexual expression continues.

But, of course, you do not have to leave town to find plenty of examples of our sex-crazed culture. A doctor friend of mine, who works in student health at a major university, assures me that this preoccupation with sex cuts across all socio-economic, racial and cultural lines. What is so disturbing, she says, is that even after being treated for sexually transmitted diseases, these educated young adults cannot imagine not being in a sexual relationship at any given time and feel no shame for contracting a "social disease." Instead, most students console themselves through irrational thinking. These "serial monogamists," as my friend calls them, do not think of themselves as promiscuous because they are always "in love" with only one person at a time. Their only concession to reality is reflected in their increasing use of condoms and birth control.

Distortions of reality like those described by the student health doctor are a standard feature of any unethical lifestyle. Because none of us can tolerate for long an acute awareness of our own faults, all of us tend to rationalize our behavior from time to time. Some, however, take these rationalizations to extremes. Scott Peck, in *People of the Lie*, his classic study of evil, pinpointed lies, half-truths and distortions of reality as the stock-in-trade of thoroughly evil people. The only way people like Stalin or Hitler can live with themselves, according to Peck, is to create their own fantasy world. This world is characterized by a belief in their own perfection, which puts them high above the rest of humanity. In this way, they can justify anything, no matter how vile. They reason that because of their innate superiority, they cannot be held to any conventional moral code and they cannot be defeated. In other words, these pathological narcissists have made *themselves* the absolute value. They are unbelievably persistent in their efforts to sustain the illusion of perfection and must shift all blame for mistakes and failures to others. Their vision of their own superiority will allow no other course. Even while causing untold human suffering, they continue to see themselves as perfect.

But the sad truth is that all of us fit somewhere on the continuum of good and evil. None of us are perfectly ethical and all of us distort reality to some extent. The best treatment for this ailment, which used to be called sin, is to be radically honest with ourselves. Because "the unexamined life is not worth living," as Plato said, wise people learn to face up to their failings and to learn from their mistakes. They can forgive and be forgiven as real human beings in an imperfect world.

All Truth Is God's Truth

One obstacle to this kind of self-examination is that we are all blinded by unrealistic beliefs. Our beliefs are based on a combination of subjective "truths" and objective facts. The facts can be verified historically or scientifically, whether a given individual chooses to believe them or not. Truth, on the other hand, is often merely personal or subjective. A given person or "subject" may believe, for example, that his parents love his sister more than they love him. He can never know for certain because his parents' minds, like all minds, are unknowable to a large extent. All he can do is gather factual evidence and then decide whatever he wants to believe. When he arrives at his own version of the "truth," he may well have totally misjudged his parents' feelings. I do not recommend torturing yourself like this, but a lot of us base our worldview and self-image on similar speculations that cannot be proven one way or the other.

This confusion about the difference between objective facts and subjective truths figures largely in the on-going argument – completely unnecessary and needlessly destructive of community, in my opinion – between science and religion. Some religious fundamentalists are unwilling to even look at the claims of science. They would rather cling to their own subjective truths than risk invalidating some of their beliefs through the examination of objective facts. Like the "liberal fundamentalists" who insist that all values are relative, they do not want to go through the emotional pain of rethinking the beliefs that comfort them. And it should be noted that by refusing to examine any facts that challenge their beliefs, religious fundamentalists and liberal ideologues are just two sides of the same coin.

A far healthier approach for religious people is to view all truth as God's truth. When scientific discoveries lend ever greater support to the theory that life gradually evolved over millions of years, faith is not well served by a refusal to examine the evidence. It is far better to let faith, which is based on the trustworthiness of God, carry us through times of doubt and questioning. By faith in the God of all truth, beliefs can be thoroughly examined. Otherwise, our beliefs become boxes that we live in, blocking our view of truth and fact, both spiritual and material.

Not even scientists are free from this kind of blindness. In *God and the Astronomers*, Robert Jastrow writes of the initial reluctance of scientists to accept the Big Bang theory of the universe's origin. At the time, the predominant belief of astronomers was that the universe had always existed, more or less in its present form. The new theory, based on evidence that the universe is expanding, seemed to prove that the universe began as a "cosmic egg" containing all of the matter in the universe. This very small, but infinitely dense, point of origin was "without form and void," as the earth is described in the book of Genesis. Then, the universe exploded into being, eventually forming stars and planets throughout the vastness of space. Most scientists hated the whole idea. Even Albert Einstein resisted the evidence of a beginning, writing, "Such possibilities seem senseless." In the words of Jastrow, "There is a strong ring of feeling and emotion in these reactions. They come from the heart, whereas you would expect the judgments to come from the brain. Why?" He explains it this way: "The scientist has scaled the mountains of ignorance; he is about to conquer the highest peak; as he pulls himself over the final rock, he is greeted by a band of theologians who have been sitting there for centuries."

Regrettably, human beings have a tendency to react emotionally when our beliefs – or theories – are challenged. Rather than thoughtfully examining new facts in the light of old truths, many of us will either deny the facts or reject the truths. We will even turn away from some of our most cherished values as we are swept up in a kind of cultural stampede, and like simple herd animals, leave destruction in our paths.

In *The Great Disruption*, Francis Fukuyama describes the way Western cultures have reacted to new technologies. Through the presentation and analysis of mountains of research, he attempts to show that our shift toward a post-industrial, information age society and medical advances like birth control were the main catalysts for the disruption of society, starting with marriage and the family. In a span of forty years, traditional values and customs were abandoned, as we reacted to the new "truth." With birth control, sex was separated from marriage. Since women could earn their own living without fear that an unwanted pregnancy might derail their careers, divorce became much more feasible. Many began to think of fathers as unnecessary. The freedom of the individual to live life on his own terms became the highest good, with the costs of these changes falling "disproportionately on the shoulders of children."

Tragically, most of these disastrous changes came about through mostly good intentions and unquestioning faith in some very questionable beliefs. We conducted, on a societal level, an experiment testing the limits of personal freedom and equality. Now the results are in and many are trying to find a way to regain what we have lost.

Self-defeating Beliefs

We cling – sometimes irrationally – to our beliefs for a variety of reasons. Adults often hold on to "trouble-making" beliefs they picked up as children because the beliefs make them feel "at home." According to Hugh Missildine, M. D., author of *Your Inner Child of the Past*, all of us carry around an inner child who continues to think, feel and experience life as we did as children. For example, a person raised by perfectionists will put himself down with messages that say "No matter how hard I work or how well I do, my efforts are never good enough." By self-belittlement, he carries on the family tradition. Another adult who was overindulged as a child will expect to be pampered and taken care of unless circumstances force him to learn to fend for himself. Beliefs such as these are at the root of much misery in adulthood and effectively block the way to happiness. Until they are discovered and challenged, they will distort the adult's perception of reality and put a serious strain on all his relationships.

Many of our self-defeating beliefs are tied directly to cultural values. The high value placed on feeling good all the time leads us to accept beliefs that lead us away from personal growth and the achievement of our greatest goals. For example, a woman who wants the kind of true love that implies a life-long commitment will never find it until she learns how to be alone without being lonely. She is too desperate. However, a belief that "if I am in love with the man of the moment, it will not be wrong to have sex with him" permits a woman to think of herself as moral and to satisfy her immediate emotional needs. Unfortunately, such neediness is not pretty and drives away the very kind of man she most wants to meet, leaving her to complain that all men are opportunistic jerks who just want to go to bed.

Psychiatrist Murray Bowen spoke of the predicament of such people when he observed, "A self is more attractive than a no-self." To be a self, as Bowen calls the authentic, confident individual, is to have well-thought-out values. When one does the hard work of thinking through her values, she will never again be tempted to assume a "no-self" position in a relationship. A self, which is neither selfish nor selfless, is inherently ethical. This means that she places a high value on *mutual* respect and personal responsibility. In the area of sex, she will not lose her self to find her man. While romantic love may remain a high value, it will never be placed above doing what is right.

A Matter of Priorities

It should be clear to the reader by now that I believe we can have every good thing as long as we put them in the right order. In fact, I believe that the surest way to find romantic love, to achieve financial security, a degree of social status and power, and to enjoy life to the fullest is to make ethical living our first priority.

What I have not made clear in my discussion of values and the way they compete with one another is that *even the ethical values have to be prioritized.* It is possible, in other words, to make a sin out of virtue.

For much of my life, I thought that to say a person was "honest to a fault" was to compliment him on his character. I did not think about the damage that one does when he says too much. In many cases, honesty competes with caring and feelings are hurt needlessly. On the other hand, it is very possible to "kill them with kindness." Every week, I deal with students who have been led to believe that it is better to feel good about themselves than to experience the temporary pain of guilt that is essential to much personal growth. Their parents have been so concerned about their children's "self-esteem" that they have failed to teach them to feel bad about bad behavior. But, as psychologist John Rosemond says, "Nobody ever changed his behavior without first feeling bad about it." And why would you?

The Biblical statement on this topic is "Speak the truth in love." In this way, it is possible to honor both caring and honesty at the same time. Still, taken to extremes, either value can do great harm.

Fundamental and Supplemental Values

Loyalty, friendliness and persistence are examples of what I call supplemental ethical values. Unless they serve more fundamental ethical values, they can just as easily support vice as virtue. Loyalty, when appropriate, is an essential part of trustworthiness. But a person cannot truly be said to be trustworthy unless he is also honest, reliable, keeps his promises and has integrity. That is why gang members, however loyal to one another they may be, will never be seen as trustworthy until they rise above the standard of "honor among thieves." Friendliness is often posted in elementary schools as an important character trait, and it certainly is a part of caring. But friendliness by itself is no indication of character. I imagine the Las Vegas prostitutes are reasonably friendly. Likewise, the telemarketers that call me on a weekly basis are superficially friendly, but I am not sure they are all honest And so, it is of utmost importance that we draw distinctions even among those values that are generally thought of as ethical.

For this very reason, I am a champion of the Six Pillars of Character chosen by the Josephson Institute of Ethics as the essential ethical values to teach our children. I believe that the diverse committee of leaders from both secular and religious youth-serving organizations who chose these values did a commendable job. It has been ten years since they issued their *Aspen Declaration* proclaiming these values as fundamental, and I do not believe anyone has compiled a list that rivals it. Because of the way these values were chosen – by consensus, the Six Pillars have an authority that most other lists of values and character traits do not. When I promote these values at school, I feel confident that every loving parent supports my efforts.

In saying that these values are fundamental, I do not intend to give the impression that I mean that any of them are **absolute.** The argument of ethical anarchists that there are no absolutes is correct, as far as it goes. Since all values compete with one another, no one value can be placed above all others as the absolute or ruling value. Ethical values like the Six Pillars of Character are better defined as **universal** – standards of behavior taught in all cultures and religions. From a theological standpoint, God is the only absolute good. Theologians refer to God as the Ultimate, the Absolute, and as the Ground of All Being. The point here, is that whatever we make our absolute or highest value, we worship. That is probably the reason that Jesus spent so much of his time arguing with the religious leaders of his day. They had made the Mosaic law an absolute and had developed it into an absurdly intricate tangle of do's and don'ts. Jesus saw that it was nothing more than an elaborate scheme for self-justification and was really a clever type of idol worship. They were serving their man-made law in the name of God.

Ethical Decision-making

To help us cope with the ethical dilemmas that confront us, wise people through the ages have developed a number of systems for making right decisions. Michael Josephson combed through these various systems, took what he thought was best and synthesized them into an ethical decision-making model that works well. With his system, making ethical decisions may not be as easy as one, two, three, but there are three steps.

First, consider the **stakeholders** and honor the Golden Rule. The stakeholders are all of the people who will be affected by your decision. Once you have identified them, treat them the way you would want to be treated.

Second, honor all Six Pillars of Character, when possible. In most cases, it is possible to be trustworthy, respectful, responsible, fair, caring and a good citizen all at the same time.

But in those circumstances where the ethical values do compete, it becomes necessary to go to step three. Step three is to think about what would be best in the long run. For example, I believe that in the long run, a child's character is more important than a so-called need to feel good about himself all the time. Discipline, from the root word disciple, means to teach, and teaching often involves correction. Sometimes that correction may hurt a child's feelings for a short time. That seems unkind and uncaring to some modern parents. In the long run, however, the child will be better off because he will form the habits of a person of character. Therefore, a parent who chooses to discipline understands that her responsibility requires that she provide her child with both love and limits. She will honor the value of responsibility over that of kindness, as needed.

Subjective vs. Objective Values

The Six Pillars of Character provide objective standards of behavior. Therefore, ethical choices are never a matter of subjective opinion. If someone lies, the objective fact is that she was not honest. If she calls someone a rude name, she was disrespectful. If she does not rein-in her appetites, she is irresponsible. For this very reason, counselors and therapists, for all of their attempts to represent themselves as value-neutral, cannot help recommending personal responsibility and mutual respect to all of their clients eventually. Once they have done that, the cat is out of the bag. Next they find themselves confronting their clients with questions like, "Were you being honest with her?" Or "Was that fair to him?" Before they know it, their clients see that they do indeed have their own moral, or at least ethical, point of view. While they may not dictate moral rules to their clients out of respect for their autonomy, they cannot do their jobs without a discussion of ethics.

Self-definition

We define our characters by the values we love most dearly. Those values lead us to habitually say and do things that determine the shape of our lives in a continuous process of interaction with other individuals, with our families, friends and other groups. To be a person of character, we must make sure that these defining values are really the ones that are worth fighting for. Are our core values and beliefs well-thought-out and intentionally chosen? Or, are we majoring on minors? Are we selling our souls for tinsel? Are we building our house on rock or on sand?

Character Is Destiny

"Human nature has been sold short...[humans have] a
higher nature which...includes the need for meaningful work,
for responsibility, for creativeness, for being fair and just,
for doing what is worthwhile and for preferring to do it well."
- Abraham H. Maslow

Scott Peck, author of *The Road Less Traveled*, once spoke in
Columbia, South Carolina on the topic of emotional and spiritual
growth. He expressed his irritation at the way so many people
excuse all sorts of bad behavior with the comment "It's just human
nature." "You know what human nature is?" he asked. "It's going
to the bathroom in your pants." He waited for the laughter to
subside and for the absurdity of the "human nature" argument to
sink in, and then, continued. "It is also learning *not* to go to the
bathroom in your pants." Perhaps out of love for our mothers, who
cannot seem to understand how convenient it is to just *go* whenever
we feel like it, all of us learn - sooner or later - to use the potty.
Humans, he argued, are capable of learning and growing, and are
much more than genetically programmed and environmentally
conditioned animals. Because we are endowed with the power to
make conscious choices, we have an incredible amount of freedom
to shape our own destinies.

Other great thinkers have emphasized the significance of our
power to choose. Viktor Frankl, a Jewish psychiatrist imprisoned in
a Nazi death camp, found that he had little or no control over the
brutality of his physical circumstances. He slept on a flea-ridden
mattress, had very little to eat and was constantly persecuted by both
his guards and many of his fellow prisoners, who believed that they
needed to steal food to survive. But Frankl refused to become like
his oppressors and tried to find some good in his situation. He
noticed that the prisoners who were surviving were not the ones who

stole food from other prisoners. Why, he asked himself, would people who stole extra food die *sooner* than those who had less?

He and his friends had decided to be kind to one another and to share both their food and their suffering. Perhaps, Frankl reasoned, by choosing a meaningful attitude toward their predicament, they had regained some control over their lives. While the Nazis had almost total control over what happened to Frankl's body, they could not prevent him from deciding for himself how to think. After the war, he used his experiences as the basis for a new branch of psychology he named logotherapy, which emphasizes our ability to find meaning in even the worst circumstances.

In later life, Frankl objected to the modern tendency to think of humans as nothing more than highly evolved animals. "While I agree that humans are a collection of drives and instincts," he said, "I will never agree that humans are *nothing but* a collection of drives and instincts."

While there is no denying that humans are a part of the animal kingdom, it is also true that we have a god-like ability to consciously choose either good or evil. The glory and the meaning of life lie in choosing the good. The tragedy is that so often we choose what is bad for us and for those we love. As a counselor, I see people every week who are making themselves miserable by making self-destructive choices, which they usually do not recognize as choices. They see their problems as completely outside of their own control. They never ask, "What's my part in this problem?" Instead, they ask, "Will you talk to my child (my husband, my wife) and get them to change?" Denying their own freedom to choose, they ensure that nothing will ever change. Their unhappy lives are proof of William James' observation: "The hell to be endured hereafter, of which theology tells, is no worse than the hell we make for ourselves in this world by habitually fashioning our characters in the wrong way." It is as if they would rather be miserable for life than face the temporary pain of self-examination necessary to change their characters and their fates.

A Life Worth Living

There is a logical progression in the development of a person's character. In character educational circles, the progression is described something like this:

> Your thoughts become your words.
> Your words become your actions.
> Your actions become your habits.
> Your habits become your character.
> And your character becomes your destiny.

Whether that character forms the basis of a hellish or a happy life depends most of all on a person's willingness to examine himself. For character, and eventually, destiny are the products of beliefs, attitudes, values and habits that make each of us unique. People with weak or bad characters have mistaken beliefs, negative or selfish attitudes and destructive habits. Also, they place a higher priority on non-ethical values than on ethical values. In contrast, people of good character have realistic beliefs, positive/meaningful attitudes and habits based on ethical values, which they put before non-ethical values. Instead of "self-esteem," they possess the more substantial trait of self-respect that comes from doing your best and doing what is right.

We Co-create Each Other

Of course, there is one problem with the idea that "a man's character is his fate" (Heraclitus) and that is that none of us are free from the influence of family and culture. Patricia Feigley, who teaches family systems theory, stated this bluntly to me once when I was going on a little too enthusiastically about personal responsibility: "There's no such thing as free will." Pat, an excellent therapist, did not elaborate on this, forcing me to think. Her point, I believe, was that the "togetherness force," as it was dubbed by the father of family systems theory, Murray Bowen, is always in tension with the "individuality force." Bowen observed that all animals, including humans, are strongly affected by these two forces. People who are better able to be their true "self" are much more successful, both in pursuing their own goals and in relationships. These people have achieved a high level of what he called differentiation of self. In common language, this means that they have well-thought-out beliefs, attitudes, values, and guiding principles and have formed habits consistent with their thinking. They define (differentiate) themselves in relationship with others by what they say and do in a *continuous process* rather than in a single statement or act. The more fully differentiated the person, the less she needs the approval or agreement of others and thus, the more able she is to direct her life's course.

Angelo

The complex interplay between an individual's character and the influence of his family and community can be seen clearly in the life of a student I will call Angelo. I met Angelo when I was co-counseling a group of high school students, who were at-risk of dropping out. Many in the group were belligerent and disrespectful and seemed to lack any motivation to grow and change. But Angelo was different. When others were rude, he remained calm and refused to be drawn into a conflict. He was very "centered." In other words, he acted like he knew who he was and where he was going. I had no doubt that he would graduate.

Toward the end of the year, I had a chance to talk to him alone, and he told me his story. Like the majority of African-American children born today, he was the child of a single mother. He had met his father once, but had no relationship with him. Even though he was quite intelligent, he had not worked in school because good grades and study were seen as "acting white" in his community. In fact, he told me that the biggest obstacle standing in his way was the fact that graduating from high school would make him different. "If I graduate, I will be the first one in my family – ever." Still, he was determined to succeed.

His turn-around had been dramatic. Just the year before, Angelo had been running with a bad crowd. Without any effective adult men in his life, he had joined a gang for a sense of belonging and to test his manhood. Loyalty to the gang was the only meaningful value he held. When the leaders told him to steal, he stole. When they told him to fight, he fought. One night, he and his best friend, Rashad, were ordered to steal beer out of a convenience store. They were to sneak it out the back door while another gang member distracted the clerk. But their scheme didn't work. The storeowner caught them and confronted them with a gun. A struggle ensued and Rashad was shot. "He died in my arms," Angelo told me in a trembling voice.

This incident forced Angelo to reexamine the direction of his life. The absurdity of a belief that taught that pursuing success in school was "acting white" became obvious. Did that mean that to be black you had to fail? He began to question his value system and recognized the folly of making loyalty to a gang his highest value when that loyalty had cost him his best friend. On some level, he knew that he was made for more than that. If he were ever to become the person he was created to be, he would have to learn to think for himself and to live by higher principles, even if that meant that he would sometimes stand alone.

The Power of Character

The power of character that changed Angelo's life is available to everyone. As Michael Josephson puts it, "Nothing about character is hereditary. Everyone, regardless of social background, financial status, race, or sex, enters the world with an equal opportunity to become a person of great or petty character." Throughout history, people have thrived in less than ideal circumstances due to the strength of their own characters. Think of the millions who survived the Great Depression and went on to achieve wealth and success undreamed of by their ancestors. Many of that generation attained a meaningful attitude that minimized their poverty, summed up by the common statement, "We didn't know we were poor." But the tough times readied them for opportunities to come.   By dint of their strong characters, they succeeded according to their values, with money quite high on the list. Determined – Scarlet O'Hara-like – to never be poor again, they set a course and reached a level of financial security that is the envy of the world. Their example proves the adage: "Successful people do the things that unsuccessful people are not willing to do. "

And so, it all comes down to a matter of will.   Limited though it may be, the power of each individual to change his circumstances is formidable. We may not be able to "have it all" – the narcissistic fantasy of our times, but we *can* choose to find meaning and contentment in every area of our lives. It is a difficult thing to achieve, but it does lie within our power. The only question is: "Are we willing to pay the price?"

Fit to Be Free

"I think of a hero as someone who understands the
degree of responsibility that comes with his freedom."
- Bob Dylan

In *The Struggle To Be Free,* pastoral counselor and teacher Wayne E. Oates tells of his lifelong struggle to be free from threats to his personal freedom in order "to put into action what God has destined that I be and become." If we will let it, something is always waiting out there to enslave us, according to Oates. He sees the values of our particular culture, some of our beliefs about ourselves and the togetherness pressure to agree with the party line and to approve of all the actions of our particular group as the main battlegrounds of the human spirit. Born into a family of mill workers, this gifted man's toughest battle was not his fight to escape from poverty, but to get beyond the values and beliefs of poverty. He wrote, "Poverty is far more than simply not having money, goods, and luxuries. Poverty is a way of life which, when once learned, is very difficult to unlearn. Poverty is a system of distrust of authority. Poverty is a system of temporary alliance between men and women which results in children, but the men are unable to contribute to their support. Poverty is a value system that shapes people's group behavior and casts out the members who do not conform to an unspoken code. Poverty has a subculture language system that reinforces a sense of kinship." In this first chapter of his book, Oates details the specific values of poverty which, even more than the very real exploitation that the poor are subject to, keeps people poor. He makes a compelling case that without the right values, no one can be free.

The values of poverty and enslavement, as Oates lived them, taught that life was "us against them." Anyone who was higher up in the social hierarchy was to be distrusted. This applied not only to the supervisors at the mill, but also to anyone who had more of anything. To collaborate with a more affluent person was seen as "kissing up" and as "forgetting your raising." To be open to educat-people was to be "too big for your britches" and to believe that you were "better than anybody else." Appealing to loyalty as a higher value than personal success, his family demanded that he shut out even the schoolteachers who were committed to helping him.

Another feature of poverty that Oates highlighted is that it is a woman-centered system. Quoting *Peasants,* sociologist Eric Wolf's book on the subject, Oates wrote that such "matri-focal" units are common in "economically depressed urban groups." Oates own family fit this pattern perfectly. In fact, all of the men in his family "exited" when the responsibilities of raising and supporting children became too great.

Family systems theory also predicts the development of emotional, if not physical, distance on the part of men in matriarchal families. The emotional unit of the traditional family system is seen as a triangle consisting of a mother, a father and children. Relationships in the extended family are described as a web of interlocking triangles. In matriarchal families, women and children are on the inside position of each triangle. Men are on the outside position. Women, who are the *overfunctioners* in such families, gain power by overfunctioning. Men tend to accept their place as *underfunctioners* as long as the "free" service they receive is adequate and until the inherent inferiority of such a position becomes so intense that they react – sometimes violently. Eventually, most of them leave the home, either voluntarily or by removal through the legal system.

A third value of poverty as described by Oates is a resistance to being told what to do. "All I have to do is take my last breath and die," his family members would say. This value of independence caused his mother to quit her job often, which meant that the family moved a lot. It is a pattern I see in the lives of otherwise intelligent students who are behind in school. When parents value their pride more than the needs of their children, they burn their bridges at one job or at one school and then, *have* to move.

In Oates' family, this so-called independence was so pronounced that his mother and brothers insisted on no set hours for work so that they could come and go at will. This is a value of people who have confused liberty with license and who believe that freedom should be unlimited. A person who tries to live like this ensures that he will be cut-off from other people because his demands are so unreasonable. And according to Bill Meynardie of Manpower, people like this are nearly unemployable. Employers, he says, are looking for the three A's: attendance, attitude and aptitude. While they may have the aptitude to do a fine job, the attitude of the chronically poor is uncooperative and counterproductive. And if they only show up for work when they feel like it, they are of little use to most employers. They may be suited for jobs that last only two to three weeks. But after that, they usually quit or get fired.

A final value of poverty identified by Oates is directness of speech. My own father, a child of the Depression, had hung onto this value of poverty and passed it on to me. Even though he became a successful businessman and genuinely loved and enjoyed most people, he would say whatever came into his head. The unusual thing about Daddy, though, was that he was always surprised when anything he said was heard as hurtful. The person had "taken it wrong" and didn't understand that he liked them. For this same reason, it has been a life-long struggle of my own to rein in this tendency to say whatever is on my mind, wherever and whenever I want. I have to remind myself that honesty is not always the best policy and that my immediate reactions are often poor representations of my true thoughts and feelings.

Oates concludes his essay on the values of poverty by acknowledging that "the poverty system has enough freedom from self-discipline and responsibility to make the poor prefer their bonds to the struggle for freedom from poverty." He quotes Rousseau, who said, "Slaves lose everything in their chains, even the desire of escaping from them; they love their servitude....Force made the first slaves, and their cowardice perpetuated it." Perhaps this attitude is what Martin Luther King, Jr. was referring to when he said that to be free he first had to remove the slavery from his mind.

The Values of Success

Dr. Oates makes it clear that it is impossible to enjoy the blessings of freedom without first making the values of freedom our own. While few of the readers of this book will be able to relate to the more extreme values of the chronically poor, all of us have been influenced by modern political movements that have emphasized rights over responsibilities and encouraged us to think of ourselves as powerless victims. These forces have led many to believe that they are entitled to be taken care of by others, and so, they waste valuable time and energy demanding their "rights." If, on the other hand, we understand that each of us has tremendous power to shape his own destiny, we will begin to take full advantage of our freedom. Knowing that the choices we make each day have long-term consequences, we will be careful to invest our time and energy in activities that build our futures. Rather than trying to shift our responsibilities to others, we will be eager to take full responsibility for our lives in order to possess the abundant life known only by those who are truly free.

Trust and Trustworthiness

"To be trusted is a greater compliment than to be loved."
- George McDonald

It is interesting to me that everyone who thinks deeply about human problems eventually comes to the conclusion that they are systemic rather than individual problems. In his insightful book *Trust*, Francis Fukuyama talks about the myth of the rugged individual in America. He shows how America's success has been a peculiar combination of independent initiative and cooperation between groups. Americans, he says, are remarkable not only for their independence of mind, but also for their tendency to form associations with people of common values and goals. He says that throughout our history, most of these groups have shared a common religious or ethnic heritage and worries that we are regressing into a more fragmented society of isolated individuals seeking more rights and fewer duties. Without shared values and a commitment to something higher than selfish interests, America may be losing the "social capital" of trust necessary to any free society.

Trust is the key element missing from many would-be democracies around the world. Fukuyama has written extensively about the role of trust in enabling democracy and capitalism to work. Carefully analyzing the cultures of various countries around the world, he has found that the level and scope of trust varies considerably from country to country. He theorizes that countries like China and those with Latin Catholic origins are lacking in trust because they have been dominated by a centralized and arbitrary state. These authoritarian governments discourage and often persecute those who would form the kind of associations that bridge the gap between family and community. Therefore, trust in China and many Latin Catholic countries is frequently limited to family alone. Many people have no loyalty to those outside the family and feel little guilt about cheating them. This makes the development of Western style democracy and a free market difficult. Imagine giving your credit card number to an internet service in a culture where people only feel obligated to be honest with family. In America, on the other hand, it is assumed that these anonymous electronic salespeople will be honest. We trust them both because honest and fair dealing with everyone is part of our value system and because we know that our legal system does not favor those who cheat in business. Whether honesty is one of the salesperson's character traits or not, he or she understands that "honesty is the best policy" and that "good ethics is good business" in the United States of America.

The ethical values of democracy encourage the formation of numerous associations to work for the common good. Groups like Little League, the Boy Scouts, educational groups and, especially, religious groups bring people together in ways that government never can. Unfortunately, membership in such groups has waned in recent years as Americans have begun to take individualism to the extreme. By turning away from our core values and from the associations that foster connections outside the family, we risk losing the trust that binds us together.

Building Trust

One of the great struggles in my own life has been my quest to find a sense of community in the various neighborhoods and towns where I have lived as an adult. Growing up in Tupelo, Mississippi, where everybody knew almost everybody else, I felt that I belonged. But in the bedroom communities of America's cities, that sense of belonging has been hard to come by. It wasn't until I moved to a small town, just a few years ago, that I found that the opportunity for connection is still available.

One of the benefits of a small town lies in the lack of anonymity that is so often decried as a deficit. Yes, it is true that everyone knows your business. Frankly, I was shocked the first time I drove up to the local laundry and was met by a lady who held out her hand and said, "Teresa Baggett, light starch." Since my wife had been there many times, they knew what she wanted; but how did they know who I was and what my car looked like? Still, that kind of familiarity is nice when the people can be trusted.

People also behave better in smaller communities because of this familiarity. Scotty, who managed the stables next door, befriended me when I first moved to Blythewood and soon became one of my favorite people. A genuine person of character, Scotty advised us on setting up our own horse pasture and barn and was always available when we "city slickers" needed a little assistance with one of the challenges of country living. In addition, he gave us advice about life in a small town. The best thing he ever told me was this: "Now, don't you make anybody mad in Blythewood. Because not only are you gonna see 'em again, you gonna see 'em *this week*." He also explained to me that it was a bad idea to gossip about anybody. Chances are, you would be talking to one of their relatives or their best friend.

There are several conclusions I have drawn from my experiences in this small town. The main one is that it is good to be connected with the people in your community. When you see people every week, you have a chance to observe them. You learn that the teenager in the baggie pants is really not the hoodlum he appears to be, and the teenager learns that if he gets too far out of line with community standards that someone will call his parents. You learn about the people you cannot trust as well and make appropriate distinctions rather than distrusting everyone. Also, you learn that you may have more in common with someone of another race and social class than you do with some members of your own family.

My relationship with Scotty is a case in point. Scotty probably has a lot less education than I do. He certainly has a lot more muscles and practical know-how than I do. He is fearless as well as strong. Once, a horse tried to kick him and he caught its leg just above the hoof. Then, he held the leg in mid-air until the horse started trembling. "It never tried to kick me again," he said. I am neither that brave nor that strong. However, these differences between us are wiped out by our shared values. Scottie is kind, helpful, respectful and generous – all traits I aspire to and admire. That is why we are friends. The rest does not matter.

My point here is that community is not possible without trust and trust is only possible when people are trustworthy. As we strive to become a global community, we must share more than modern business practices and the mechanics of capitalism.   We must reeducate ourselves and try to educate our potential business partners in other countries about the ethical values of democracy that build trust.

To Be Worthy of Trust

Trustworthiness is one of the six bedrock values of a good character.   **Trust** is an attitude and a precious commodity that results when people in a nation, community or family are worthy of trust. A complex value, trustworthiness is a combination of honesty, reliability, promise-keeping, loyalty when appropriate, and integrity. While supplemental values like honesty and loyalty are often used to justify unethical behavior, the fundamental value of trustworthiness is not so easily perverted.   Though an "honest" journalist might spread destructive gossip with a clear conscience, a trustworthy one never could. Gangs make loyalty their highest value and use it to excuse every kind of dishonorable behavior, but young men and women who are truly worthy of trust find better ways to belong.

I often hear youth leaders urging young people to trust one another as if trust were the character trait we are trying to develop. This approach encourages a kind of blind faith in others and shows a lack of understanding about how character is developed.   In my attempts to help middle schoolers stay focussed on the worthiness of their own actions, I have looked for common experiences and re-framed them in terms of character. With that in mind, I wrote an article for the school newsletter that featured the "trust fall," which is an important part of our school's ropes course.

The Trustworthiness Fall

Everyone who has been through the BMS ropes course remembers an element known as the trust fall. For those of you who don't know, this is an exercise that requires you to stand on a platform - four feet high - and then, to fall backwards into the arms of two rows of teammates, trusting them to catch you. Hence the name. But could it be that by calling this challenge the trust fall, we are placing emphasis on the wrong character trait?

While it does take a lot of trust to fall, the more important value of the trust fall is found in the trustworthiness that is developed along the way. By the time you get to the trust fall, you have built a relationship with your team; and it is not by chance that this part of the ropes course comes after hours of team-building. It can only happen when every person knows that he can trust his teammates.
Both trusting and being trusted are great experiences. Be worthy of trust.

The ropes course at our school is an amazing experience. Most of the young people start out wondering if they can trust themselves, let alone their teammates, to tackle all of the tasks they are asked to master. But before it is all over, they have done things as a team that they did not think possible - including taking a stroll on the catwalk, thirty feet in the air. They learn not only teambuilding skills, but also problem-solving, critical thinking, and leadership. In fact, many students who do not shine in the classroom emerge as leaders in tackling these practical challenges. And so, in addition to trust, they develop mutual respect, responsibility and courage.

Trustworthiness has been a hallmark of American society, and in spite of our differences, is a matter of pride for most Americans. Just think of all the movies that have featured the story of the motley crew of diverse individuals who save the day by pulling together and learning to trust and respect one another. It is a popular theme because it is our story. Truthfully, it is impossible to imagine America without the contributions of citizens from every ethnic, religious and racial group. We need to remember what they did and appreciate the roles trust and, especially, trustworthiness played in making their contributions to our nation possible.

The Siamese Twins of Freedom

"That government is best which governs least,
because its people discipline themselves."
- Thomas Jefferson

Thomas Lickona, the influential author of *Educating for Character,* identifies respect and responsibility as the other two R's that need to be taught in schools in addition to reading, writing and 'rithmetic. These Siamese twins of freedom work in tandem to regulate our rights to life, liberty and the pursuit of happiness. Unfortunately, our worship of tolerance and other less fundamental values has led us to neglect the teaching of these essential character traits and the social skills that go with them. Mr. Lickona notes that since the time of Plato, wise societies have wanted their children to be not only smart, but good. But many Americans today act as if being smart is the only thing that matters. In the education reforms sweeping the nation, the emphasis is on academic achievement for children and accountability for educators. Teachers are expected to be over-responsible and to respect and tolerate all kinds of "cultural" differences, but children are only expected to get good grades and to score well on standardized tests. In this version of America, all children are above average and come from perfect homes. Therefore, if some children fail or misbehave, it must be the fault of teachers or some "disorder" that educators are expected to accommodate. We have forgotten Theodore Roosevelt's caution that "To educate a person in mind and not in morals is to educate a menace to society." When violence and drugs enter our schools, we scratch our heads and wonder why. But to those of us who work in public schools, the reason for the breakdown in civil order is obvious. When students are pushed to excel in sports or academics at any cost, when they are taught that equal achievement is their due, when they are taught that the highest good is to have freedom without limits, when they are protected from the consequences of bad behavior and outright laziness, when the responsibilities of students and parents are shifted solely onto the shoulders of educators, children fail to develop the respect and responsibility needed in a free society.

In writing for the school's *High Voltage* newsletter, I have tried to help students and parents see that our freedom consists of the choices we make and the consequences of those choices. The way we learn to be responsible is by experiencing consequences that help us understand that freedom, responsibility and personal power are all part of the same package. When students finally understand that both their negative and positive consequences are the result of their own choices, they become empowered to take control of their lives. However, in our "nation of victims," as it has been dubbed by author Charles Sykes, parents and teachers are fighting against a tidal wave of popular culture and outrageous court decisions that tell our children that stuff just happens and no one is ever responsible – unless they have "deep pockets." Then, of course, they should be sued for all a jury will award.

This is not to say that we are fighting a losing battle. Many, many loving parents refuse to let their children be swept away by the current of culture and are eager for any insights that might help them carry out their own responsibility to teach the values of democracy.

Freedom, Responsibility and Trust

What teenagers want most, according to Mike Gannon of the Department of Juvenile Justice, is freedom from adult supervision. And, he says, they will do almost anything to get it, including behaving responsibly in order to earn their parents' trust. A parent's main task is to set limits on their children's freedom until they prove that they can handle it responsibly. Children who cannot be trusted to act responsibly under any circumstances, have to be supervised by an adult at all times. They have no freedom from adults at all. On the other extreme, children who always make good choices can be

trusted with almost complete freedom. Parents of such children simply have to make sure the environment the children are
in is safe.

As young people mature, they should be earning more
and more freedom until they are finally ready for the
responsibilities of adulthood and all of the rights and
privileges that come with it. By making the connection
between responsible choices, trust and increased freedom,
they become self-disciplined and no longer have a need for
adult supervision - which, incidentally, leaves their parents
free for other pursuits. It's a win-win situation.

To clarify my own thinking on the responsible, respectful
exercise of freedom, I turned to the words of one of our nation's
greatest leaders, Abraham Lincoln.   In his Pulitzer Prize-winning
book, *Lincoln at Gettysburg,* Garry Wills masterfully illustrates
Lincoln's ideas on the meaning of liberty. At Gettysburg, Lincoln
identified *The Declaration of Independence*, not *The Constitution*, as
the seminal document on which our country was founded. The key
passage, of course, is:

> "We hold these truths to be self-evident; that all men are
> created equal; that they are endowed by their Creator with
> certain unalienable rights; that among these are life, liberty,
> and the pursuit of happiness."

Unfortunately, the majority of Americans have not spent
very much time thinking about the meaning of this statement.
Instead, they have reacted emotionally and allowed themselves to be
directed by the popular culture, largely abandoning their own principles. As a consequence, we have developed a culture that is often
unethical and seriously out of touch with reality. On the one hand,
we emphasize equality without any reference to freedom; and on the
other, we claim unlimited freedom without recognizing how free-

dom competes with equality. Lincoln didn't make this mistake. In a wonderful passage discovered by Wills, he wrote:

> "I think the authors of that notable instrument [the Declaration] intended to include *all* men, but they did not intend to declare all men equal *in all respects*. They did not mean to say all were equal in color, size, intellect, moral development, or social capacity. They defined, with tolerable distinctness, in what respects they did consider all men created equal – equal in 'certain inalienable rights, among which are life, liberty, and the pursuit of happiness.' This they said, and this they meant."
>
> (italics and brackets are Garry Wills')

If you accept Lincoln's analysis, you will begin to see how America took a wrong turn somewhere along the way. The promise of America is an equal right to life, liberty and the *pursuit* of happiness, period. It is not the promise of perfect equality in all things, neither is it the promise of unlimited freedom without regard for the equal freedom of others. But in modern America, we try to have it both ways. Our children are inundated with messages proclaiming, "No Limits." Or, "No rules, just right." Are we really surprised that they hear "Have it your way" as an entitlement? This very selective emphasis on equality alone on one occasion and on freedom alone when it suits us has led our nation far away from the founders' most basic value of equal freedom for all people. The ideal of equal freedom grew out of ethical values, such as respect, responsibility, fairness and justice. Equality divorced from freedom is inherently unethical and is based on envy as much as anything else. Unlimited freedom is the narcissistic dream of toddlers. Neither value, by itself, leads toward the formation or maintenance of an ethical society; and, as I have noted before, democracy is an ethical movement. Without ethics, injustice abounds and true democracy is lost.

It is quite a challenge to communicate such lofty concepts in terms that adolescents can understand and doubly difficult when they live in a culture having an identity crisis of its own. However, I sometimes find that I can apply the wisdom of great leaders like Lincoln to everyday situations in a way that anyone can appreciate. The following article is a good example:

Equal in Freedom

We live in a country based on the belief that all people are created equal, but how are we equal? Abraham Lincoln thought as deeply about that question as anyone in history. In the years leading up to the Civil War, he wrote that of course we are not "equal in color, size, intellect, moral development, or social capacity." He concluded that what we are equal in is freedom and that every person has an equal right to exercise his freedom. In other words, every middle school student has the same freedom as any other middle school student. Every adult has the same freedom as any other adult – no more and no less.

As Americans, we have to learn that equality sets limits on freedom and that the only way to show respect for the freedom of others is by limiting our own. For example, I don't play loud music in my house after my wife has gone to bed. I respect her right to go to bed earlier than I like to. I limit what I say, especially when I am angry, because I do not want to force others to deal with my emotions. It's my job to handle my own emotions. And so, equal freedom demands that you and I consider other people before we speak or act and that we take responsibility for our own thoughts, feelings and actions. It requires self-discipline and that does not come easy. But then, character is not for wimps. It is only for the tough-minded. Keep struggling.

Just as equality sets limits on freedom, freedom set limits on equality. Students who choose not to work or study will never achieve equally with students who do. In reality, they are free to fail. But in our politicians' minds, ideology is more powerful than reality. The new No Child Left Behind legislation, holds educators, not students, responsible for underachievement. In fact, a careful reading of the law reveals that not only will educators be expected to motivate all students to learn, but they also will be expected to see to it that all students achieve on a proficient level, which is the equivalent of a B average. Like the children in Garrison Keillor's mythical town of Lake Wobegon, all children in America are now – officially – above average. Despite the fact that 25% of them fall into the slow learner range of intelligence or below, educators are mandated to ensure that both those who are unwilling and those who are unable to achieve at a high level succeed anyway. According to this legislation, Lincoln was dead wrong. We *are* equal in all respects, after-all.

Ages and Stages of Freedom

Children's preparation for life in a democracy starts long before school age as they begin to learn self-control from their parents. When, at around the age of two, children first notice that some people have the temerity to tell them "No," most fly into an impressive rage. My own daughter, who is one of the most strong-willed people I have ever known, used to be able to sustain one of these fits for a full two hours. Once thwarted in her attempts to get into something that was off-limits, she would fall at our feet and begin to howl. Simply stepping over her and ignoring her, which had worked like a charm with our son, had no effect. She would quickly get up, follow us to our new position and throw herself at our feet again. Then, she would commence to scream and beat her head on the floor with renewed vigor. We endured these marathon screaming sessions two or three times before we realized that, "Hey! We can put her in her crib and shut the door." Once placed in her crib, she realized that she was only hurting herself and soon calmed down. Instead of a two-hour "hissy fit," she merely fussed for ten minutes.

These early experiences helped my daughter accept the fact that she was not the center of the universe. Just a year later, she was still mischievous and full of energy, but instead of constantly fighting with her parents, she had fun with her need to test her boundaries. After spying some forbidden (dangerous or breakable) item, she would reach toward it, grin at her mother and say, "Is it off lemons, Mama?" Although she had not yet mastered the English language, she had already gained some mastery over her own awesome temper.

My nephew demonstrated the other major preoccupation of toddlers when he was visiting my house a few years ago. While there, he expressed an interest in one of my daughters old toys and she presented it to him as a gift. Then, his mother prompted him with the familiar parental phrase, "What do you say, Chandler?"

"Mine," he replied, hugging the gift tightly to his body.

The crisis for toddlers is summed up in these two words: "No" and "Mine." According to developmental guru Erik Erikson, these "terrible twos," as I like to call them, are swinging back and forth between a sense of autonomy and deep feelings of doubt and shame. In other words, they are preoccupied with their own freedom and with the boundaries of that freedom. Parents must respect children's need to establish their own boundaries by providing them with both love and reasonable limits. As we get older, we continue to define our boundaries, to test our limits and to flex our muscles of freedom, so to speak. The issues get more complex, but the task is essentially the same.

We set our boundaries by asking:

1. What am I willing to do and what am I unwilling to do?
2. What will I put up with from other people and what will I refuse to put up with?
3. What is mine and what is yours?

In the exercise of our freedom, these are the crucial questions. To answer them correctly, we must learn that our freedom is no more than equal to that of other people our same age.

As we get older, the limits on our freedom should get broader and looser as we prove that we have the maturity to discipline ourselves. The problems come when some of us act as if we have no limits on our freedom at all.

Limits, Safety and Respect

The Johnson Institute of Minneapolis has been studying the problem of youth violence and has uncovered some facts that they believe point the way to a more civil society. Concerned about the increase in bullying and other violent behavior in American schools, they researched the beliefs, feelings, attitudes and behaviors of those who bully, of their victims and of the adults who are charged with keeping the peace. What they found was that rather than beings victims of low self-esteem, as is sometimes suggested, bullies have abnormally high self-esteem and feel **entitled** to bully to get what they want. Not used to hearing the word "No," bullies spend their days threatening, spreading rumors, calling names, pushing, shoving and hitting. If adults are doing their jobs, they can severely limit, if not stop, this violent behavior. But too often, adults do not want to get involved, are intimidated themselves, have misguided beliefs about the bullies not feeling good about themselves, value **tolerance** as an absolute and do not understand how much power they have to end violence in all its forms. When adults tolerate bullying in this way, victims feel that they have nowhere to turn and have the potential to become violent themselves, either by attempting suicide to escape their torment or by fighting back.

The Institute defines violence this way: "Violence occurs whenever anyone inflicts or threatens to inflict physical or emotional injury or discomfort upon a person's body, feelings, or possessions." Most significantly, he identifies any kind of disrespect as a form of violence. When we show disrespect for a person, we are crossing their boundaries. For example, degrading comments about a person are often experienced as threats to that person's self-concept. We know, instinctively, that one of our inalienable rights is the right to define ourselves. When someone tells a nasty rumor about us, they are attempting to redefine our characters for us. And that is something that most of us are willing to fight about. We can fight in a disrespectful way or a respectful way, but we will not take such slander lying down.

Adults can make schools and communities much safer by taking seriously their role as limit-setters in society. David Wilmes points out that wherever adults set the limits, children will push three to five steps beyond those limits. That is just human nature. Think of the way most adults drive. We have all heard that the highway patrol will not give you a ticket if you are only going five miles over the speed limit. So, most of us begin by going five miles over. An interesting exercise is to ask responsible adults how fast they think they can drive without getting stopped. I have been doing that for awhile and so far, the consensus seems to be that you can go up to nine miles over the highway speed limit before you are likely to be stopped for speeding. My point here is that the way we find out what our limits are is to push them. When state troopers on the highway are lenient, we speed. When adults are lenient, children bully other children. Therefore, youth violence is really an adult problem. Adults who choose to be tolerant are clearly **enabling** bullies and discouraging those who are respectful and well-behaved. As Ayn Rand put it, "It is obvious who profits and who loses by nonjudgmentalness. It is not justice or equal treatment that you grant when you abstain equally from praising virtues and condemning vices. When your impartial attitude declares, in effect, that neither the good nor the evil may expect anything from you, whom do you betray and whom do you encourage?"

The Problem of the Pecking Order

People who work with animals have long observed that this problem of bullying is not peculiar to humans. When we refer to the "pecking order" at work or at home, we are using a phrase - coined years ago - that first applied to chickens. Back in the good old days (for birds) when all chickens were "free range" chickens, farmers knew that after the rooster, there was a clear hierarchy of hens and chicks. The top hen could peck any bird except the rooster. The hen under her could peck everyone below her and so on down the line until it got to some poor chick that was persecuted all day long by every bird in the barnyard. I have observed this phenomenon myself since moving to the country and wrote about it for the school newsletter. Please forgive the incredibly corny title.

The Horse Who Says Nay to Disrespect

My horse, Ranger, has to work hard to maintain his dignity. As the horse on the bottom of the pecking order in a two-horse pasture, he is bullied everyday. When I go out to the barn at feeding time, he has to wait until Royal, our little mare, walks into her stall. She will not allow him to enter the barn first under any circumstances because we have taught her (or perhaps, she has taught us) that the first horse into its stall is the first one fed. But once she is in her stall and locked in, Ranger has a chance to demonstrate that he is still his own man. Instead of walking straight into his stall, he often walks right past it and circles the barn at least once before going in - twice, if he feels particularly insulted. He knows that I will not feed Royal until both horses are in their stalls. Royal knows it, too.

What is this all about? I think it is a demonstration of a principle well known by human psychologists. They have observed that no one is willing to stand in a position of inferiority; and that when people are treated with disrespect, they will get back at the person who has put them down in some way. Ranger's actions are an excellent example of what is called passive-aggressive behavior. While he would never engage Royal in an actual fight, he loves to frustrate her and he knows just how to do it. He seldom makes any aggressive gestures at all until he is safely behind the bars of his stall. Then, he often backs his ears and acts like he is going to bite her. She makes faces back at him. It is all quite silly, but not all that different from some human behavior. But the good news is that people are smarter than horses and can learn how to get along.

So, show respect for everyone, no matter his or her position in the herd, and we can put an end to biting, kicking and other unpleasant behavior.

While it is undeniable that humans are much more than mere animals, it is also clear that we do have what Saint Paul referred to as a lower nature that drives most of our unethical behavior. As a part of our animal nature, it is quite natural for humans to put each other down as a way to handle individual anxiety. Our continuing challenge is to rise above our animal nature and to make respectful and responsible behavior a habit that becomes "second nature."

Thoughtful Responses vs. Emotional Reactions

Adults have a duty to teach the young how to stop, cool down and think about their values before saying or doing anything in a tense situation. One story I occasionally tell my students illustrates how keeping your head can get you out of trouble and even put you in charge. It happened when my brother and I were young adults and went to check on some horses he was keeping in another man's pasture. As we were leaving, we got a little unwanted attention from the gentleman's bull. It lowered its head and pawed the earth. Being the coward I am, I slowly backed out of his way. But being the cowboy he is, Rick decided to play matador. He jumped at the bull, causing it to charge. Then, he ran backwards until the bull stopped. Thinking this was great fun – and to my dismay, he did it again and again.

Unbeknownst to us, the next door neighbor of the rancher had been taking this in and was headed our way – thoroughly outraged. Suddenly, from behind us came a stream of profanity as this fellow proceeded to tell us what idiots we were. Turning, I acknowledged the man and he then decided to vent all of his anger on *me*. I told him that I agreed with him and had been asking my brother to stop. He replied that I was a blankety-blank and wasn't doing enough. Meanwhile, my brother had stopped his foolishness and was listening closely. His loyalty to me was causing him to build up a considerable rage himself. As he walked toward the man, he had every intention of smacking him in the face. But something happened to him as he approached the barbed-wire fence separating us. He had time to think. When he reached the aggrieved neighbor, he stuck out his hand mechanically and said, "I'm Rick Baggett and you're right. What I was doing was really stupid." And then the miracle occurred. This stocky, scary-looking man melted. His whole posture and facial expression changed from one of rage to one of remorse. To my complete surprise, he apologized to both of us and explained that the bull had already torn through the wire and gotten into his pasture twice before. But, he admitted, that was no excuse for the way he had talked to us. Though I had always heard that "a soft answer turns away wrath," I had never seen it happen so dramatically.

When I tell students this story, I am trying to help them see that showing respect for others is a position of strength. As Rudyard Kipling put it,

> "If you can keep your head when all about you
>   Are losing theirs and blaming it on you…
>
> Yours is the Earth and everything that's in it,
>   And – which is more – you'll be a Man, my son!"

One of my students learned this lesson the hard way, after he failed to keep his cool. Another student, who I consider to be an expert at provoking others, persisted in telling nasty rumors about this young man. Finally, Fred confronted him in the gym and a fight ensued. Both boys were suspended from school for three days. During that time, Fred received counseling from a friend of the family that was quite meaningful to him. Returning to school, he sought me out to share what he had learned. It was such a good story that I asked his permission to write about it in the school newsletter. He agreed and the following article is the result.

The Strongest Man

*"It is curious - curious that physical courage should be
so common in the world, and moral courage so rare."*
- Mark Twain

A young man was being counseled by one of the wise men of his faith community. He had acted impulsively and had gotten into serious trouble. In a firm voice born of love the older man asked, "Who is the strongest man?"

The young man shrugged, then guessed, "The one who can lift the most weight?"

"Oh no," the wise one replied, "it is the man who can hold his own anger."

As Black History Month comes to an end, it is important to remember that the victories of the civil rights movement were won primarily because the protesters were able to hold their anger to achieve a greater good rather than seeking the short-term satisfaction of getting in their licks. They simply and bravely sat down at "white only" lunch counters and tried to order a sandwich. And then, when they were abused - physically and verbally, they sat quietly and waited to be arrested by the police. In this way, they respectfully demanded the equal rights they deserved, and no person of conscience could resist the power of their courageous stand.

Equal Respect between Men and Women

"No one will ever win the battle of the sexes.
There is too much fraternization with the enemy."
- Henry Kissinger

One of the great controversies of our time has centered around men's and women's roles in the family and in society. For almost forty years, we have struggled to redefine these roles. During this time of transition, we have often fought bitterly, leaving

many casualties along the way – children and families chief among them. But our difficulties are understandable. Because hierarchy is necessary to any well-functioning group, human or animal, we have trouble thinking in terms of equal partnerships and shared power. Someone has to be the boss, we say. Therefore, someone is always in a "one-down" position. Even in our families, we talk in terms of men "wearing the pants in the family" or as being "hen-pecked."
Growing up as the son of a man who actually announced, "I am the master" from time to time, I myself had quite a struggle translating the ideal of equality between the sexes into reality in my own marriage. But fortunately, I married a woman who understood and lived the concept of *mutual respect.*

Teresa, a pediatrician, is a humble person, but a strong person. In our marriage, we worked together to overcome cultural stereotypes that shaped our own expectations in spite of our beliefs and values. Conflicting messages about a woman's place or a man's place presented challenges for us as we attempted to define ourselves as a couple. Teresa had to contend with guilt about being a good enough mother and wife when her job forced her to be away from home more than the average woman. She also fought against the pressure to "have it all" by refusing to accept additional positions on important boards and committees that would take her away from the family even more. I worried that having less income than my wife made me less of a man and that keeping children as much as I did was not "natural" (and by the way, I am convinced that it "ain't natural" for a man to keep small children for long periods of time). But because respect, responsibility, marriage and family were among our highest values, we toughed it out. We did what was right even when it felt wrong. As a result, we have a marriage that is resilient and strong. We have been through the fire.

It is unfortunate that so many couples cannot seem to work out the stresses of their lives together so that everyone wins. Placing too high a value on individual freedom and fulfillment, men and women often put their own needs and wants above those of the person they say that they love. Unable to tune out the insistent voices of our secular culture, they seek relationships that will somehow complete them without asking them to change in any way. As Gloria Steinem so aptly put it, "There are many more people trying to meet the right person than to become the right person." But when we see character traits like respect and responsibility as something for the other person to work on, we throw away our chance for happiness together.

The Christian community's response to the changing roles of men and women has been disappointing to me. Reacting emotionally rather than responding thoughtfully, out of Christian principles, many conservative churches have demanded a return to the 1950s when "men were men, and women were glad of it." More liberal churches, on the other hand, have thrown out the baby with the bath water, accepting whatever alternative lifestyles the culture has produced. Since I have already written quite a bit about the folly of making such tolerance an absolute value, I would like to concentrate now on the problems created by the conservative churches when they take rigid positions on the roles of men and women. I would like to show that any effort to treat women as less than men is not in the spirit of Christ and to encourage serious Christians to consider the Bible's teachings on this subject more carefully and thoughtfully.

One of the best statements on Jesus' attitude toward women was written by Dorothy Sayers, the British author of the Lord Peter Wimsey mysteries and of many essays on Christianity. In a short book entitled *Are Women Human?*, she summed up her thoughts on Christ's model like this:

> Perhaps it is no wonder that the women were first at the Cradle and last at the Cross. They had never known a man like this Man – there never has been such another. A prophet and teacher who never nagged at them, never flattered or coaxed or patronized; who never made arch jokes about them, never treated them either as "The women, God help us!" or "The ladies, God bless them!"; who rebuked without querulousness and praised without condescension; who took

their questions and arguments seriously; who never mapped out their sphere for them, never urged them to be feminine or jeered at them for being female; who had no axe to grind and no uneasy male dignity to defend; who took them as he found them and was completely unselfconscious. There is no act, no sermon, no parable in the whole Gospel that borrows it pungency from female perversity; nobody could possibly guess from the words and deeds of Jesus that there was anything "funny" about woman's nature.

Anyone who is familiar with Jesus' life knows that his treatment of women is one of the things that so infuriated the leaders of his day. Israel was a strict patriarchy. Men held all the cards. Jesus challenged all of that. He objected to the quickie divorces of His day and said that when men divorced their wives for any reason other than adultery, they themselves were committing adultery. In fact, He told these self-righteous fellows that even to look with lust at another woman was to commit adultery in one's heart. He talked to women like Martha and Mary with the same respect accorded His disciples. Furthermore, His teaching that all of us are sinners put us all, men and women, on an equal footing. We all need forgiveness. We all need a Savior. Therefore, Jesus ministered not only to the tax collectors and other male sinners, but also to prostitutes and adulteresses.

After Jesus' death, his disciples carried on his message about equality between the sexes, however imperfectly. Saint Paul, who is so often misused and taken out of context to support the subordination of women in the Church, wrote one of the most radical statements ever made on the subject of equality in his letter to the Galations. In the *New International Version*, Galations 3: 27-28 reads: "for all of you who were baptized into Christ have clothed yourselves with Christ. There is neither Jew nor Greek, slave nor free, male nor female; for you are all one in Christ Jesus." In other words, for the Christian there is no race, no social class and no gender; we are all equal before God.

To say that we are all equal is not to say that we are the same, however. Many of Paul's writings that are misinterpreted deal with problems created by the differences between the sexes and with those unique to particular churches at particular times. Writing to new churches in very diverse cultures, he sometimes laid down rules that seem sexist to modern ears. Most famously (or infamously), he advised that the women in Corinth should "remain silent in the churches." If they had any questions about the sermon, they were to wait and ask their husbands about it at home. Because the Corinthians were attempting to practice Christianity in an area where the major religion was a fertility cult, dominated by women who shaved their heads and acted as temple prostitutes, Paul wanted there to be no confusion about the differences between the two cultures. In addition to his demand that women take a passive role in the services, Paul asked them to refrain from cutting their hair as well. Women with long hair, who remained silent in worship, could not be mistaken for temple prostitutes. Considering the special circumstances, at a time and place where Christianity was a poorly understood, new religion, Paul's requests seem quite reasonable. But it does not follow that all women today should remain in the background and should always let the men lead. Such a teaching is not Biblical.

Of course, men are not the aggressors here and it is probably just as common for women to be the primary decision-makers in a family as it is for men. To understand how things really work, I have had to retrain my thinking away from a strict either/or, good/bad interpretation of family and societal functioning. In most cases, the person who leads the family at any given time is simply filling a role that is demanded by the family *system*. It is not an individual choice. As I have already stated, all well-functioning systems have a hierarchy. Problems only develop when that hierarchy becomes too intense. Then, we are tempted to use words like "pecking order," "abusive," "domineering" and so on. Family systems therapists refer to the power structure in family in very neutral terms. The person who takes a little more than his/her share of responsibility for the family is called an *overfunctioner*. One who takes less than his/her share is an *underfunctioner*. Most of the time, this recriprocal relationship between overfunctioning and underfunctioning works quite well. For example, in my own family, my wife overfunctions when it comes to planning vacations. Because she works so hard all year, the thought of vacation gives her hope. Therefore, she plans our vacations at least a year in advance and studies guidebooks and travel magazines as a hobby. This preoccupation of hers also suits her temperament. Teresa is one of those people who likes to be very organized, to have all her "ducks in a row," as she often says. I, frankly, am an underfunctioner in this area and enjoy flying by the seat of my pants sometimes. After the initial discussion about where we want to go, I leave much of the how to her. I do whatever I need to do to support her efforts, but she is definitely in charge.

In well-differentiated (emotionally mature) families, each adult may overfunction to some degree in one area and underfunction in another. That is balanced and fair. Overfunctioning and underfunctioning become troublesome only when balance is lost. Again, it is a matter of intensity. When overfunctioners (men or women) become tyrants and underfunctioners (men or women) stop contributing to the family altogether, family members become symptomatic. Spouses use more and more conflict or emotional distance to manage their anxiety. Rather than relying on each other for emotional support, they increasingly press children or one particular child, into service as an "emotional spouse." While conflict, emotional distance and emotional triangles are functional relationship patterns in most families, they create any number of problems when overused in this way. Overfunctioners burn-out, underfunctioners become increasingly "disabled" and some family members get sick, act out or develop emotional illnesses.

The only answer for a family that has fallen into a rigid pattern of overfunctioning and underfunctioning is for both spouses to commit themselves to the practice of equal respect and personal responsibility. They must learn to *show* respect for other people even when they do not respect their actions. Also, they must learn the difference between being responsible *to* one another and being responsible *for* one another. This will require them to endure the anxiety that accompanies any significant change. And it will require great patience because systems change very slowly. But given time, they do change. Eventually, respectful, responsible speech and behavior become automatic and yes, natural.

Equal Respect between Adults and Children?

I understand that the way people work out the issue of equality in marriage is a very personal thing. However, I thought it was important to address because children learn how to respect other people and to take responsibility for themselves more through observation than by what they hear. As the saying goes, "Children will not always do what we say, but they will never fail to do what we do." If they see that mother or father is treated disrespectfully, they will assume that it is right or, at least, the norm for someone in the family to act as a boss who runs roughshod over everyone else. And so, they will seek a position of either dominance or submission in their relationships and may never learn how to assert themselves in an ethical way that allows everyone to keep their dignity. Suffice it to say that parents are by far the most important influence on a child (an obvious point for those who work with children on a daily basis) and that in most cases a child's character is simply a reflection of the parent's. Therefore, it is crucial that parents treat one another with respect and behave responsibly themselves.

The issue of equal respect between adults and children is a thorny one today and has become a source of confusion for many. Some adults have become so uncomfortable with their responsibility to teach children how to behave and with the inherent "inequality" of such a relationship that they have sought ways to avoid their duty to children altogether. Depicting themselves as little more than large children, they have tried to erase generational boundaries by instructing children to call them by their first names and by trying to be their "friends." But of course, children do not really want adult friends. They want parents and mentors. Friends are people with a similar level of emotional maturity. Adults with the maturity of children are to be avoided at all costs. Hence the confusion. Still, it is a touchy subject in an age when we are constantly told to treat everyone equally. So, how can we show respect for children and, at the same time, expect them to respect our authority over them?

When we ask children (or adults) to "respect authority," we are asking them to respect the right of adults to set limits, expectations and rules of behavior in the areas for which they, as adults, are responsible. In other words, we do not respect people in positions of authority such as our parents, teachers or supervisors at work any more than we respect anyone else. We are all created equal, after all, with the same dignity and worth. But we do respect the authority of those people to be in charge of their *sphere of responsibility*. A teacher, for example, must set rules for the classroom for which he is responsible. If there is a lack of discipline in his room that prevents some students from learning, he is accountable for it. And so, he has a legitimate right to exercise his authority over the pupils he teaches. In the same way, parents are responsible for teaching their own children how to behave and so, have legitimate authority to discipline.

Notice the relationship between responsibility and freedom. Those with more responsibility have more freedom of choice than those with less. For some, this is an inducement to pursue areas of ever-expanding responsibilities. The more responsibility, the more freedom and power. It seems like a good bargain. For others, however, this is a fine reason to give up as much personal freedom as possible. If I am not free to make many choices, then I am largely "free" from responsibility.

Of course, there are plenty of adults who have no intention of respecting children in any way, shape or form. The opposite of the adult "friend," who attempts to deny the differences between adults and children, is the adult who sees herself as "the boss." This is the kind of person who enjoys bullying others and feels entitled to do so in her position of authority. She has no respect for a child's real need to think for himself, to learn to manage his own emotions and to make choices, however limited. The boss is much more interested in punishment, with its goal of justice, than with discipline and its goal of education. Respect to this person simply means respect for authority. She has no concept of respecting children as individuals who are equally valuable as human beings.

An emotionally mature adult can be a "leader" rather than a friend or boss. This type of person is both **demanding** and **responsive** to children. She respects them as being equal in dignity and worth, but understands that she has a responsibility to discipline them that sets her apart from them. She never betrays their trust by being a mere "friend" and never puts them down as inferiors, as a "boss" might do. And because she understands that "it takes character to teach character" (Josephson), she examines herself to make sure that she communicates her rules and expectations in as respectful a way as possible.

Parenting for Character

Teaching children respect and responsibility is not easy, but it is fairly simple. All that is required is that we provide children with:

1. **Unconditional love.** This is often confused with un-conditional approval, but it is something quite different. Unconditional love means to have goodwill for our children even when we do not like them. It means that we show respect for our children even as we hold them accountable for their actions. And it means that we sacrifice any amount of time and energy to give them whatever they truly need – including the discipline needed for good character.

2. **Clearly defined and strictly enforced limits.** Many adults confuse children by failing to clarify their expectations and by being inconsistent in enforcing their

rules.   By using values like trustworthiness, respect,
responsibility, fairness, caring and citizenship as our
standards, it becomes much easier to define acceptable
behavior and to use our legitimate authority to discipline.
We can give children choices based on our values and
teach them that their choices matter by seeing to it that
they experience the consequences of their actions.

3. **Freedom to move within the limits.**   Children must
    have opportunities to exercise their freedom by making
    choices.   The mistake of "boss" parents, is to have so
    many rules that children feel that the only way to have
    any autonomy is to disobey. Ironically, study after study
    has shown that extremely authoritarian parents raise
    children who are every bit as undisciplined as children
    raised by permissive parents.   Because "boss" parents
    provide little opportunity for children to make their own
    choices, their children fail to develop the self-discipline
    that only comes from experiencing the consequences –
    both positive and negative – of one's own choices.   In
    contrast, parents who lead rather than boss their children
    give choices within limits. And if they are wise, they err
    on the side of caution in setting those limits,
    understanding that it is part of human nature to push our
    limits. In other words, they know that to have a teenager
    home by midnight, you may need to give them an 11:30
    curfew.   The recommendation of developmental
    psychologists is that parents should strive to be "slightly
    more than moderately strict." Beyond that, we reach the
    point of diminishing returns where excessive rules and
    strictness provoke an uncooperative spirit in children.
    This stands to reason since humans have a natural
    reaction against any unnecessary restraints on freedom.

Choose with Care

All Americans must learn to make respectful, responsible choices. By making these values our guiding principles, we will maximize our own freedom without infringing on the equal freedom of others. And we will move our nation a little closer to the realization of our dream.

What Is This Thing Called Love?

Perhaps the greatest casualty of our culture's war over values has been Love itself. Indeed, we no longer even know what the word love means. Does it mean the same thing to say that you love your Lexus or your cell phone as it does to say you love your mother? Is there any difference in "free love" and the type of love practiced in those marriages that last a lifetime? Do we really love our children when we diligently attend to their self-esteem without any concern for their souls? Wendell Berry, an author often described as prophetic, writes that we have forgotten that the "feeling of love" is not equal to the "practice of love." The practice of love that supports "marriage, family life, friendship, neighborhood, and other personal connections" is characterized by "trust, patience, respect, mutual help, forgiveness" – in other words, by ethical values and by the attitudes cultivated by living ethically. And so, when people say that they just want to be loved, what they really mean – whether they know it or not – is that they want to be loved ethically.

Loving ethically is not promoted by our culture. Our culture is based on consumption and we are a nation of consumers. We are in a regular panic to buy and try out new things. If it cannot be owned, it should at least be experienced, we feel. Most of these products and experiences are sold by advertisements that appeal to basic instincts (our lower nature) and so often that means that sexuality is devalued and used to "pimp" (Berry's apt word) for whatever is being sold. As long as it supports the economy and the license that we have mistaken for liberty, we think it must be all right. We try to ignore the gnawing emptiness inside ourselves, our families and our communities, or else, to fill it with more things, newer experiences or more satisfying people. In our pain, we wonder if love is just an illusion anyway.

CHARACTER COUNTS! attempts to get around our confusion by substituting the word "caring" for love as one of its Six

Pillars of Character. I think that was wise since love means so many different things to different people. At least caring implies an ethical love and is not easily confused with lust, greed and other base values that so often masquerade as love. The ancient Greeks also recognized this confusion and dealt with it by creating a variety of words to designate particular kinds of love. C. S. Lewis, in *The Four Loves,* states that three of these are "natural" and spring from the emotions. Only one has the power to transcend nature and is enabled by God's spirit at work in the human will. According to Lewis, the natural loves were also created by God and were meant to be enjoyed, but they can only bring happiness when they are submitted to the ethical (righteous) values that embody God's Love.

The instinctual loves described by the Greeks are *Storge* (affection), *Philia* (friendship) and, of course, *Eros* (sexual love). Each is important and adds much to our lives, but none of them lead, necessarily, toward the kind of ethical love that keeps families, friendships and communities together. Affection for a person, place or thing may lead one in the direction of true love. It certainly is a lot easier to sacrifice some of your time, energy and resources for a person (animal, forest) when you feel affectionate. However, we often feel affection for people and things for all the wrong reasons. We may like a fellow because he always brings the drugs to the party; laugh at a friend's put-downs of others; and enjoy vulgar music, violent movies and anti-social video games (a new one offers the "fun" of shooting women). Therefore, indiscriminate affection can carry us into some dark places. Friendship tends to move us in a positive direction, but we all know of the danger of "falling in with a bad crowd." We warn our children that "you are known by the company you keep" and "birds of a feather flock together." But overall, we think of friendship as a very good thing. Although it may not rise above the level of "you scratch my back and I'll scratch yours," friendship usually inspires some spirit of giving in us. The giving may be rather self-serving, but at least it starts us thinking about the welfare of others. Sex, the third of these emotional forms of love, is an astoundingly powerful force to bind people together for a time and for the propagation of the species; but it cannot take the place of genuine love. While it is certainly useful for reproduction, it is of no use in raising the children produced and is a flimsy basis for marriage. Helen Fisher, in *Anatomy of Love: a Natural History of Mating, Marriage, and Why We Stray,* states that the hormones that are activated when we "fall in love" do not last. Her mostly anthropological research indicates that the typical period of erotic infatuation ends after only four years. When marriages abide "until death us do part," something more substantial than hormones is at work. And so, *Eros*, like affection and friendship, fails the test of true love precisely because it is merely a feeling that comes and goes. For us to move beyond the ephemeral feeling of love to the enduring practice of love requires a commitment to what the Greeks called *Agape*.

Unlike the emotional forms of "love," *Agape* is a love of the will. Henlee Barnette, my professor of Christian Ethics at the Southern Baptist Theological Seminary, taught that to love with *Agape* means "to will the well-being of all Creation." Because God created all things and every person on earth and pronounced them good, we should also love everyone and everything on the whole earth. In my own thinking, I still reserve the right to hate certain viruses and bacteria, fire ants and crab grass. However, I may be wrong even in that. When it comes to despising human beings, I know I am wrong. To lump certain groups of people together as hateful – rich people, poor people, politicians, whoever – is sinful. To hope for some evil to befall a person who has mistreated and abused me is also quite the opposite of love. And yet, I catch myself doing these things from time to time because I am human and in need of forgiveness and *Agape* myself.

Jesus and the prophets understood that it was not enough to say, "Love one another." People need specifics. Otherwise, we will find ways around such vague advice. When the Pharisees - experts in the law - came to Jesus and asked, "Teacher, which is the greatest commandment in the Law?" Jesus took the opportunity to spell out what we are supposed to do and who we are to do it to. He quoted their own scripture: "'Love the Lord your God with all your heart and with all your soul and with all your mind.' This is the first and

greatest commandment.   And the second is like it: 'Love your
neighbor as yourself.' All the Law and the Prophets hang on these
two commandments." (Matthew 22: 34-40, *NIV*) Luke 10: 25-37
describes a similar conversation Jesus had with a Pharisee who
seemed to be looking for a loophole. After being told to love his
neighbor, this Pharisee replied, "And who is my neighbor?" Then,
Jesus told the famous story of the Good Samaritan:

> "A man was going down from Jerusalem to Jericho,
> when he fell into the hands of robbers. They stripped him of
> his clothes, beat him and went away, leaving him half dead.
> A priest happened to be going down the same road, and
> when he saw the man, he passed by on the other side. So
> too, a Levite, when he came to the place and saw him, passed
> by on the other side. But a Samaritan, as he traveled, came
> where the man was; and when he saw him, he took pity on
> him. He went to him and bandaged his wounds, pouring on
> oil and wine. Then he put the man on his own donkey, took
> him to an inn and took care of him. The next day he took out
> two silver coins and gave them to the innkeeper. 'Look after
> him,' he said, 'and when I return, I will reimburse you for
> any extra expense you may have.'"
>
> "Which of these three do you think was a neighbor to
> the man who fell into the hands of robbers?"
>
> The expert in the Law replied, "The one who had
> mercy on him."
>
> Jesus told him, "Go and do likewise."
>
> *- New International Version*

The choice of the Samaritan as the loving neighbor was de-
liberate on Jesus' part. No other group of people was so despised by
the Jews. For Samaritans were Jews who had intermarried with
Gentiles and had been cut-off from the Jewish community. So, it
was the kind of disagreement that can get really ugly – a family
feud. In choosing the Samaritan, Jesus was saying, in effect, "Yes,

love everyone, even your worst enemy and your least favorite people."

It is interesting to speculate about who Jesus would portray as the Good Samaritan today. Depending on which of us he was talking to, he might tell the story of the Good Homosexual, the Good Republican or Democrat, the Good Single Mother or perhaps, the Good White Protestant Man. Because our prejudices know no bounds, he would have his hands full making the story relevant to all of our diverse and divided groups. But since God's love knows no bounds, we know Jesus would say that each of us is the man bleeding on the side of the road and all of us should be like the Samaritan.

The Ten Commandments provide clear rules for people who are supposed to be committed to one another's well-being and to loving God. A pastor I know once spoke of the Ten Commandments and the Great Commandments as being like ten fingers on two arms. The Ten help the Two do the detailed work of love. Four of the Ten tell us how to love God; six deal with loving our neighbor. First and foremost is the command, "You shall have no other gods before me." Because there can be only one absolute in our lives, we must remember to give God first place. The second forbids worshipping idols, i.e., anything (money, power, pleasure, status, etc.) that we are tempted to put in the place of God. When we worship these things instead of God, we turn our backs on Him. His love cannot reach us because we are not receptive to it. The third commandment is "You shall not misuse the name of the Lord your God." Dr. Phil McCarty, my Bible professor at Mississippi College, taught that to take God's name in vain was more than simple blasphemy - as bad as that is. We misuse God's name, he said, whenever we give Him the credit or blame for something He is not responsible for. If that is an accurate interpretation, then we need to be very careful about proclaiming that our cause and God's are one and the same. The fourth commandment is "Remember the Sabbath day by keeping it holy. Six days you shall labor and do all your work, but the seventh day is a Sabbath to the Lord your God. On it you shall not do any work, neither you, nor your son or daughter, nor your manservant or maidservant, nor your animals, nor the alien within your gates." This one is very precisely worded, and yet, we manage to ignore it pretty well nowadays. God just asked us to rest and take time to remember that the meaning of our lives comes from worshipping Him and following His Way, but even that is too much for us. Everything is open "24/7" because we can no longer imagine turning down any opportunity to make and spend money or to advance our status at work. Perhaps that helps explain why so many of us now have great careers, but no time for a life. Without a weekly check on our tendency to seek our own way, we never stop to examine our lives and values. We never are still enough to allow God to speak to us about our families, our friends, our communities and yes, our work. And so, the fourth commandment, like the first three, tells us how to love God as the absolute value of our lives.

The last six Commandments, as I have said, deal with our relationships with one another. And they are in plain language. "Honor your father and mother, so that you may live long in the land the Lord your God is giving you." "You shall not murder." "You shall not commit adultery." "You shall not steal." "You shall not give false testimony against your neighbor." "You shall not covet your neighbor's house. You shall not covet your neighbor's wife, or his manservant or maidservant, his ox or donkey, or anything that belongs to your neighbor." Again, clear instructions. If you love your neighbor (meaning parent, co-worker, friend, someone on the other side of the world, etc.), this is how you will treat them. Yet, we can always find exceptions to the Law of Love. And when we cannot rationalize our unloving behavior away, we try to excuse ourselves by saying that the history of the world proves that religion does not work, anyway. But the truth is, as G. K. Chesterton said, "The Christian ideal has not been tried and found wanting. It has been found difficult; and left untried."

This little Bible study has been necessary for me because I cannot talk about the proper practice of love without thinking about *Agape.* I have to speak from a Christian perspective because that is my source of knowledge and wisdom. Also, I am convinced that, whatever your religion, the practice of love requires an act of faith. Even though it does nothing to advance our place in the social hierarchy, directly; does not get us more things; and does not guarantee us friendship, affection or sex; we are told to will the well-being of other people and the rest of Creation and just trust God. We are told to seek first the Kingdom of Heaven and that, if we do, all good things will come to us as well. We are promised "abundant life" and are assured that if we "lose" our lives in loving God and neighbor, we will "find" our lives and become our true selves. That requires a relationship with God, and so, moves us beyond mere ethics.

I frankly doubt that anyone can have this kind of goodwill, which is devoid of ulterior motives and selfishness, without an assist from God's Spirit. To love and pray for your enemies is not a natural thing to do. To want what is best for the woman you are in love with, even if her best future does not include you, is not "normal." To spend time with the poor, the sick or the grieving when you would much rather be anywhere else, is not an act of purely human love. To grant your children the freedom to become the people they were created to be when what you really want is to keep them on a narrow path of your own design requires a willingness to put them into God's hands. All of these kinds of challenges demand a submission of our human wills to something, or more to the point, Someone higher than ourselves.

Characteristics and Guiding Principles of Love

This is not to say that we can do without the other ethical values that I have been writing about. The other Pillars of Character are necessary to spell out how loving people behave. When we love someone, we are honest, loyal, reliable and keep our promises so that we are worthy of their trust. We treat them with respect and fairness and we are responsible to them. These values support the rules we know as the Ten Commandments. To a large degree, they describe righteous living. But where respect, responsibility, trustworthiness and fairness tell us how to live lawfully, love tells us how to live spiritually.

Love moves us beyond a respect that teaches us to mechanically say "I disagree with you" when we want to say "You're an idiot!" Instead, we show respect for people because we love them and understand that they need to be treated with respect in order to become the people God wants them to be. Love helps us to stop being **responsible for** perfectly capable children and to see that their real need requires that we be no more than **responsible to** them. That is, love helps us move them toward independence and a degree of separation from us that is sometimes painful for both them and us. For when we love rightly, we are committed to the personal growth (spiritual, emotional, physical and mental) of the person loved, even though they may well outgrow us.

Other important ethical values supplement love and make it more than just a word. Kindness, humility, forgiveness and patience provide a kind of evidence that our love is real. Because these traits require that we give up something (our time, our egos, our need for "justice," our tempers), they demonstrate our willingness to sacrifice for our loved one. To be kind enough to be attentive to the words or the needs of others is to sacrifice our needs of the moment for theirs. To listen to their point of view and to let them have their way requires that we put them first. To forgive someone who has wronged us or to be patient with a child who wants to "help" is a precious gift.

Some of the guiding principles of love are:

1. Be unconditionally committed. There is great wisdom in the traditional wedding vows that have us promise to take one another for better or for worse, for richer or for poorer, in sickness and in health, until death us do part. What good is a love that will not stick with you through the hard times?

2. Stay connected with extended family and neighbors. Resist the temptation to "burn your bridges" when there is a disagreement or when feelings are hurt.

3. Forgive. Part of the problem with denying our own faults in order to protect our "self-esteem" is that it leaves us no way to mend relationships. We all need to forgive and to be forgiven frequently.

4. Give of your time and attention. This gift takes many forms, but the most common need is for someone who will listen. As someone who has been trained to attend to and follow what another person is saying, I appreciate how much energy and concentration is required to listen well. But I think it is sad that so many people have to pay big bucks to a professional therapist just to be heard.

5. Sacrifice. Children need enormous amounts of time and attention from adults, not only to listen, but also for training, education and play. Unfortunately, some career-minded parents have convinced themselves that a little "quality time" will be enough. It is not. Love for children demands that we take full responsibility for giving them what they need even when it means that we have to make choices that sacrifice or postpone some of our own dreams.

6. Be non-reactive. Love takes the lead when we can stay calm. Many marriages have turned around when one spouse learned to hold his or her anger and to wait for the other person to cool off. Instead of taking everything personally, a non-reactive person can "throw out the emotional garbage" and address only the real issues.

⚖️

The Gift of Love

Love is the greatest gift to humankind. Out of love, we commit ourselves to one another for life in marriage. We give our time, attention, energy and resources to our children. We help our neighbors in times of trouble and even send money to people in other places that we do not know and will probably never meet. It allows us to forgive and love our enemies - not because of who they are, but because of who we are. It brings us peace when peace seems impossible. It heals us and makes us whole.

Recovering the American Character, Reclaiming the American Dream

"America is great because she is good. And if America
ever ceases to be good, America will cease to be great."
- Alexis de Tocqueville

In the foyer of my home is a print of "Woman with a balance" by the seventeenth century Dutch painter, Johannes Vermeer. I love this work because it symbolizes the task that all of us who would live a good life are called to do. It is a deceptively simple painting. A pregnant woman is standing before a table strewn with jewelry, gold and pearls, illuminated only by the light coming through a small window opposite her. She is facing a mirror and holding a balance in one hand. Behind her is a large painting. For many years the portrait was known as either "Woman weighing gold" or "Woman weighing pearls," and it was thought of as nothing more than a scene from everyday life. But then, people began to take a closer look and noticed details that led to an entirely different and much more meaningful interpretation. They found that although the woman is gazing intently at the balance in her hand, the pans are empty. She is weighing neither gold nor pearls. Instead, she appears to be lost in thought as she contemplates the bare scales. What could she be thinking? A significant clue is the painting behind her. It is a portrayal of the last judgement, a time when God will come to judge all people for the choices they have made. Along with the balance, which often symbolizes a judgement between good and evil, this background painting conveys the importance of weighing one's values carefully. Awaiting the birth of her child, the lady ignores the jewels before her and never glances at herself in the mirror on the wall. Instead of vanity and material goods, her focus is on other things. Whether she is reordering her priorities or rediscovering her true values, she is engaged in a process that is essential to a life worth living.

In the same way, Americans are beginning to think about the relative worth of our competing values and to question some of the

choices we have made. Has self-fulfillment through our careers become more important to us than our duty to our families? And have
we made a good bargain by accepting the "time poverty" that results
from our ever-increasing hours at work in exchange for a few more
things at home? In business, does service to our customers come
before profit or have we let the cost/benefit analysis take the place of
business ethics? Have our educators forgotten that wisdom is more
valuable than knowledge and that character is more crucial than
ability? Are we still trying to find justice amidst the competing
claims of freedom and equality through our political process or do
we simply react to the pressures of special interest groups? Can
religion still serve as the nation's conscience or is it freedom *from*
religion that we seek?

I am convinced that most of our present unhappiness is due
to either a conscious choice in favor of unworthy values or – more
likely – to confusion about what our core values are. If enough of us
will take the time to examine our private lives, we will recover those
core values and begin to reclaim the American dream – for all of us.
There is no reason that we can't. We're Americans, after all, and
our history proves that whatever we set our minds to, we can
accomplish. Let's come together and complete the work that the
founders of our nation started so long ago.

Brief Meditations On Values And Character

It's *All* About Values

Our values are the things we most highly prize and greatly desire. What we value most determines the direction of our lives and the quality of our relationships. Values like caring, respect and responsibility are called ethical values. People who make ethical values their top priority tend to have good relationships with others and to get more out of life in general. Values like money, fun, power and freedom are called non-ethical values. These values can be pursued in an unethical (wrong) way or in an ethical (right) way. For example, fun is wonderful in its proper place. But when we choose fun over doing our work, we fail to be responsible and make poor grades. When we make our fun more important than the rights of others, we damage our relationships through uncaring and disrespectful behavior.

All values compete with one another. Putting them in the proper order is the key to happiness. Seek to do what is right (be ethical) first, and all other good things will come to you as well.

• • • • • • • • • •

"Always do right. This will gratify
some people & astonish the rest."
                              - Mark Twain

"Happiness is not a goal; it's a by-product."
                              - Eleanor Roosevelt

Love Thyself

An awful lot of junk is written and said about loving yourself. Some of us suffer from a kind of false self-esteem that says, "I am going to approve of myself and whatever I do, all the time." This type of self-esteem is based on feeling good rather than doing good and being good. People who live this way do not truly love themselves enough. When they are pressured by the group to do wrong, they think, "If I don't go along with them, they won't like me." In other words, they put the group's wishes over what they know to be right for themselves. And so, they live life in a position of weakness, unable to do without the feeling of being liked. But after doing wrong, they have to put a lot of energy into **not thinking** about what they did. Otherwise, they will **feel** bad about themselves. And that gets me to my main point about love or caring.

Real love is an act of the will. Good feelings will follow and stay with you when you act in a loving way toward yourself or others, but the love itself is a chosen attitude that always results in action. For example, choosing to say "No" to so-called friends who want you to do wrong is an act of self-love. When you refuse to take drugs, you are valuing your own health and future above the temporary feeling of being liked or being high. This takes courage. When you force yourself to form better work habits, you are loving yourself as well because you are refusing to settle for a life that is less than the best. This means that love often involves self-discipline and delaying gratification now for something much, much better in the future. In other words, caring is not for weaklings; it is only for those who **choose** to be strong enough to do the sometimes difficult work of love.

• • • • • • • • • •

"In a real sense, all life is interrelated. All men
are caught in an inescapable network of mutuality,
tied in a single garment of destiny. Whatever affects one
directly affects all indirectly. I can never be what I ought
to be until you are what you ought to be, and you can never
be what you ought to be until I am what I ought to be.
This is the interrelated structure of reality.

"I believe that unarmed truth and unconditional love
will have the final word in reality. That is why right,
temporarily defeated, is stronger than evil triumphant."
- Martin Luther King, Jr.

"He who loves others is constantly loved by them.
He who respects others is constantly respected
by them."
- Mencius

"No act of kindness, no matter how small,
is ever wasted."
- Aesop

The Greatest Gift

"Rings and jewels are not gifts, but apologies for gifts.
The only true gift is a portion of thyself."
- Ralph Waldo Emerson

I learn a lot by watching other people. Many years ago during a lazy week at the beach, I learned something important about relationships by watching a father and his three young sons. Throughout the week, this Dad took great care to spend time with his boys, but he did it in a way that many of us would think was inefficient.

Most of us would play in the waves or toss a frisbee with all three at once. That way, we could get back to our summer reading quickly or maybe, squeeze in a few more rounds of golf. Not this guy.

First, he would take one boy out on the pier to fish. Later on, he would ride bikes up and down the beach with another. Finally, he would take the third son out in a sailboat. The next day, he would start all over again. The activities might change, but the pattern was the same. It was amazing the time this father wasted.

Well, I was single at the time and still young enough to think like a kid. Watching this man and putting myself in the place of his boys, I thought he was probably the smartest Dad in the world. He seemed to understand that we all crave a little bit of undivided attention now and then. I'd like to think he did the same thing for his wife.

The Caring Connection

Comedian Jeff Foxworthy likes to joke about his "redneck" family reunions. Some of his family members are so different from him that he is tempted to avoid them altogether. About all he has to say to one cousin every year is "Hey Bud, can you move your car so we can get out?" Still, it is clear that he has a lot of affection for "his people." That is the way it is with families. In families, we are connected with people in a special way that transcends differences. We will go to great lengths to help family members who do things we do not approve of and who have some crazy ideas. They may even root for the wrong team. But since they are family, none of that matters.

Staying connected with family is one of the guiding principles taught by most family therapists. Because the emotional support of family is important to our own individual functioning, calling, writing or visiting with kin is a wise thing to do. Even when they are driving us crazy, being in touch with family helps to keep us sane.

• • • • • • • • • •

"Compassion is the basis of morality."
                        - Arnold Schopenhauer

"One must care about a world one will never see."
                        - Bertrand Russell

Small Things

*"We cannot do great things in this world.
We can only do small things with great love."*
- Mother Teresa

Most Americans want everything to be bigger and better. We drive the biggest cars we can afford and live in bigger houses than we need. We even "biggie size" our meals. Rather than seeking to do our best, we strive to be perfect. And even when we reach most of our goals, we still tend to think we should be more, do more and have more. Too often we are like the Texan who was trying to impress a man from Rhode Island with the size of his ranch. The Texan, who did have a really nice place, exaggerated, "Why, it takes me two full days just to drive from one end of my ranch to the other." The Rhode Islander, in the understated way of people in New England, replied, "Yea. I once had a car like that." Looking at life through more humble eyes, the man from Rhode Island had a different view. He did not expect to be the biggest and greatest. He just wanted a car that runs. But most of us are more like the Texan.

Even when we try to serve others, we want to do something great. When someone asks us for counsel, we want to give advice that will solve the person's problems once and for all, even though most people just want someone to listen. We miss opportunities to be a small part of the food drive or to stuff envelopes for a charity because those things seem so ordinary. Anybody could do it. And yet, so few of us do. No wonder so many are hungry in a rich country and lonely in a crowd.

• • • • • • • • •

"It's a funny thing about life: if you refuse to accept anything but the best, you very often get it."
- W. Somerset Maugham

"Actions speak louder than words."
- Author Unknown

"Pretty is as pretty does."
- Billie Porter Baggett

"To think is to differ."
- Clarence Darrow

"Anybody who is any good
is different from anybody else."
- Felix Frankfurter

"To be nobody but yourself – in a world which is doing its best, night and day, to make you everybody else – means to fight the hardest battle which any human being can fight, and never stop fighting."
- e. e. cummings

"People are born equal, but they are also born different."
- Erich Fromm

Judging Erin

Over the weekend, my wife and I watched the movie *Erin Brockovich*. It is one of those films that does more than entertain; it makes you think. In fact, we were still talking about it the next day. We liked the movie, but we couldn't decide whether we liked Erin. Like many real-life heroes, her vices were just as pronounced as her virtues. It was tempting to judge her harshly.

Erin was a single mother, twice divorced, when she starting working for lawyer Ed Masry as a file clerk. With her foul mouth and combative attitude, she offended just about every one of her co-workers. All signs indicated that this would be another one of Erin's short-term jobs. But one day, she came across something that peaked her interest – health records mixed in with real estate papers. Going way beyond her job description, Erin decided to investigate. What she discovered was that hundreds of families in a nearby town were being poisoned by ground water contamination from the Pacific Electric and Gas Company and that the company was trying to keep it quiet by buying their houses. The movie chronicles her efforts to get justice for the affected families.

What Erin did for the people in her community was heroic, but her disrespectful attitude and language made her hard to love. Why was she so defensive? I found a clue in one of the deleted scenes on the DVD I rented. In this scene, George is trying to get Erin to take a break from her research. She refuses, explaining that because she is dyslexic, she has to read everything in advance. Otherwise, she'll "look stupid" when she tries to read in front of the lawyers. Obviously a very bright person, Erin has been frustrated all her life by a disability that masks her intelligence. The way she lashes out at practically everyone in her office is inexcusable, but what nobody understands is that she does so because she is hurting.

Erin Brockovich reminds us to follow Plato's advice: "Be kind, for everyone you meet is fighting a hard battle." For without the patience and kindness of her boss, Erin would never have had a chance to shine. She still might be seen as just a foul-mouthed woman who can't hold a job.

● ● ● ● ● ● ● ● ● ●

"We know what a person thinks not when he tells us what he thinks, but by his actions."
- Isaac Bashevis Singer

"We shut our eyes to the beginnings of evil because they are so small, and in this weakness is contained the germ of our defeat."
- Samuel Taylor Coleridge

"If you have knowledge, let others light their candles by it."
- Margaret Fuller

"Conscience is God's presence in man."
- Emmanuel Swedenberg

Love Rules

A popular song from the 1970s declared, "What the world needs now is love, sweet love. It's the only thing that there's just too little of." It was a typical song of the time, and most people agreed with the sentiment. If only people would love one another, everything would be wonderful, we thought. But in spite of the overwhelming public belief in the 60's and 70's that "love is the answer" or "all you need is love," the love revolution never happened. In fact, by every social indicator imaginable, Americans are less loving today than ever before. Why? Could it be that most of us have been chasing the wrong kind of love?

I believe that what we really hunger for is not puppy love, infatuation, friendship or even romance, as nice as those are. What we desire is something that lasts, something you can count on. What we need, in short, is an ethical love. This type of love is a combination of all of the fundamental character traits we call the Six Pillars of Character. Is it caring? Sure, but that doesn't say it all. Love is also respectful and responsible. It is as fair as it can be. It is certainly trustworthy because without trust, there can be no good relationships. And finally, a loving person is a good citizen who plays by the rules and does his duty toward friends, family and community. It may not sound romantic, because it is not an emotional, fickle love. It is, instead, a love of the will. As Henlee Barnette,

Professor of Christian Ethics, once said, "Perfect love means to will the well-being of all Creation." It requires a commitment to love even when the person we love is not likeable and when our circumstances together are not good. You might say it is a love for all seasons and all types of people. If we ever decide to embrace it, we will finally become the radical, counter-culture we once imagined ourselves to be.

• • • • • • • • •

"What the world really needs is more love
and less paperwork."
                                        - Pearl Bailey

"Pick your battles."
                                        - Nancy Gregory, principal

"Our Constitution was made only for a moral and
religious people. It is wholly inadequate
to the government of any other."
                                        - John Adams

"You have not lived a perfect day, even though
you have earned your money, unless you have
done something for someone who cannot repay you."
                                        - Ruth Smeltzer

"Until he extends the circle of compassion to all
living things, man will not himself find peace."
                                        - Albert Schweitzer

A Community of Caring

Author Lorraine Johnson-Coleman told a true story on public radio about one African-American woman's memories of growing up in the segregated South. It was one of those stories that is both funny and sad. The woman remembers going to town with her Daddy one day and getting very excited when she saw the water fountains. One was labeled "white," the other, "colored." She asked her Daddy, "Oh, may I please get a drink of water?" He replied, "Sure," but was puzzled by the little girl's enthusiasm. Soon, the child returned with a look of disappointment on her face. Now, she was the one who was puzzled. When she saw "colored" on the water fountain, she had assumed that pressing the pedal would produce a rainbow of colored water. Imagine the hurt she felt when her Daddy told her that the sign was there to stop black people from drinking from the same fountain as whites.

This story reminds us of a time in our country when personal morality and family values were much stronger than they are today, but social justice was neglected. In general, Americans were more trustworthy, responsible and respectful back then. In some ways, we may have been better citizens. But by failing to care about and be fair to all of our people, we created a situation that was intolerable for minorities. Without caring and fairness for all, we were not the America we claimed to be and, on some level, truly wanted to be. It took the work of a lot of caring people to pass legislation to ensure equal opportunity for all.

Our challenge today is to personalize caring for each person we meet. To do this, we have to understand that real love is not a feeling, but a choice. No matter how you feel about someone, you can choose an attitude of goodwill or caring toward them. All of us can remember times when we have cared about family members who we did not like at that moment. As people of character, we should also care about those outside our family or group - even when we disagree with them. When we do choose to "will the well-being" of everyone, we begin to create a community of caring, and that is a wonderful way to live.

• • • • • • • • • •

"You define your character by what you say and do,
especially in your relationships with others.
Every interaction is an opportunity to take
a stand for your beliefs and values.
Make sure they are worth fighting for."
- Rob Baggett

"There are two ways to live life.
One as though nothing is a miracle.
The other is as though everything is a miracle."
- Albert Einstein

"America is the only country ever founded on a creed."
- G. K. Chesterton

"There is a point at which [tolerance]
ceases to be a virtue."
- Edmund Burke

Your Habits Become Your Character

"We are what we repeatedly do.
Excellence, then, is not an act, but a habit."
- Aristotle

In the movie, *Hero*, Dustin Hoffman plays a selfish, uncaring jerk who happens to be on the scene when a plane crashes. He reluctantly saves the lives of several people by carrying or dragging them from the plane. It's not something he really wants to do, but the people won't stop begging him for help. Ironically, the media try to make him into a national hero. As the story progresses, the reporter most responsible for exaggerating his heroism gradually comes to see him as the self-centered, weak character he truly is.

This film makes some interesting points about character, heroes and celebrity. First, being famous and popular do not change who a person is, and second, the people who get most of the attention are rarely the ones who deserve it. I talk to some wonderful students every week who do not consider themselves to be popular and often feel overlooked by teachers. I try to explain to them that virtue is its own reward and that good feelings that last come from inside. That is why they call it *self-esteem*, I say. It's a tough sell in our culture of celebrity where everyone expects to have his "fifteen minutes of fame."

The final lesson I draw from *Hero* is that one act, good or bad, does not make you a good or bad person. Dustin Hoffman's character is not a genuine hero because his rescue of the air crash victims was an isolated act - unlike anything he had ever done or was likely to do again. On the flip side, one mistake does not make you a bad person. It is only when you lie repeatedly that you become a liar. One slip in a moment of weakness doesn't do it. No, bad character is the sum of a series of bad choices; and good character is the result of making a habit of telling the truth, showing respect for others, being responsible and showing others that you care. Truly, "We are what we repeatedly do."

What kind of habits are you forming?

• • • • • • • • • •

"Destiny is not a matter of chance,
it is a matter of choice;
it is not a thing to be waited for,
it is a thing to be achieved."
- William Jennings Bryan

"Self-respect is the root of discipline:
the sense of dignity grows with the ability
to say no to oneself."
- Abraham J. Heschel

Breaking Barriers

"You are never a loser until you quit trying."
- Mike Ditka

When I was a child, my play was often interrupted by a loud booming sound in the sky that reminded me of the cannon fire I had heard at the movies. It would cause me to stop whatever I was doing and squint up into the blue, searching for its source. What in the world could be making that mysterious noise, I wondered? Then one day, my father explained to me that whenever a jet broke the sound barrier, it produced something called a sonic boom. His explanation was enough at the time, but I really did not understand how it worked. Eventually, my curiosity led me to learn more about what caused the sound, why it was called the sound barrier and how it first came to be broken.

The man who broke the sound barrier was Chuck Yeager. In 1947, he was one of a handful of test pilots flying experimental aircraft designed to exceed the speed of sound. By that time, a number of young men had lost their lives in these jets and some pilots had begun to wonder if the sound barrier really was like a wall that could not be passed through. A few even wanted to quit the program. Yeager understood their fear. Whenever his Bell XS-1 approached the speed of sound, it would shake violently. Occasionally, it would spin out of control. Still, he refused to believe that the right plane flown by a competent pilot could not do what others said was impossible. Finally, on October 14, 1947, Yeager flew faster than ever before. Once again, his jet felt like it was about to explode. Then suddenly, his flight became incredibly smooth as he became the first to outrun the sound of his own plane. Through courage and determination, Chuck Yeager had "punched a hole in the sky," paving the way for the fighter pilots and astronauts of today.

• • • • • • • • •

"The real battlefield is the human heart."
- R. B.

"For everything you must do today,
you can either look forward to doing it
or look forward to getting it done."
- Ralph Marston

"The only place where success comes
before work is in a dictionary."
- Vidal Sassoon

"Whatever is worth doing at all
is worth doing well."
- Philip Dormer Stanhope

"Freedom, responsibility and power
are all part of the same package."
- R. B.

The Right Stuff

In his highly entertaining book *The Right Stuff*, Tom Wolfe tells the story of the test pilots who "pushed the envelope" by flying the first super-sonic jets and riding the first rockets into space. Men like Chuck Yeager, Alan Shepard and John Glenn had special qualities that allowed them to succeed where so many others had failed and often, died trying. They had what Wolfe referred to as "the right stuff," a combination of bravery, determination and skill that brought them world-wide fame.

We all are thrilled by feats of physical courage and are impressed by those who break new ground. What is rare to find in such a hero is the ability to put such achievements in their proper place of importance. Woodrow Dantzler is that kind of man. As Clemson's quarterback in 2001, he became the only player in NCAA history to pass for 2000 yards and to rush for 1000 yards in a single season – enough fame to go to anyone's head. But Dantzler summed-up his accomplishments in this way: "I'm really not worried about my on-the-field stuff. That stuff may fade away. What really matters is what kind of person you are." And by remembering that the most important and lasting qualities are our character traits, Woodrow Dantzler showed that he truly had the right stuff.

Cultivating Courage

One of my favorite sayings is "Mistakes are for learning." This theme reflects a certain attitude about life that says that whenever I make a mistake, I will not pout or get angry, but instead, will treat it as an opportunity to improve myself. Those who just quit when they make a few mistakes are like a man who trips and falls and refuses to get up. He says, "As long as I'm down here, I might as well spend the day." As silly as this sounds, it is no different than what we do when we fail to profit from our mistakes.

The key is courage. Children (and adults) who make mistakes need to be *en*couraged to figure out where they went wrong and to keep doing their best. Those who are defeated by failure are *dis*couraged. They are afraid to try again. "What if I study and do my homework and still make a bad grade?" they say. "That would be awful." And by "awfulizing," they discourage themselves from trying. In contrast, students who learn how to encourage themselves with positive self-talk find that they can take mistakes in stride. Like the old song, they say to themselves, "Pick yourself up. Dust yourself off. And start all over again."

• • • • • • • • •

"Guilt is good, as long as it only lasts
five minutes and produces change."
                                    - Frank Pittman

The Person I Want to Be

Sometimes a simple question will say more than a book full of facts. I recently attended a conference titled "Family Systems Symposium: Thinking That Makes a Difference." One of the speakers presented her personal struggle to have a good relationship with her troubled sister. She came to the conclusion that she needed to keep the focus on herself by asking, "What kind of a sister do I want to be?" In doing so, she found the peace that comes when we stop blaming others and concentrate on the person we do have a little control over, ourself. Then, she could begin to think about other things that she could do something about. Most importantly, she started thinking about her own guiding principles. Ethical values like respect for her sister's ability to make her own decisions and practical rules like the one I have about not staying at people's houses more than 48 hours help us stay calm. In fact, just having principles lowers your anxiety. For one thing, it limits your choices. You don't get too worried about peer pressure when you are already clear in your own mind about what you will and will not do.

I hope we will all ask ourselves similar questions. What kind of a student do I want to be? What kind of a teacher? What kind of a parent? Husband? Wife? Mother? Father? Son? Daughter? Sister? Brother? Do I want to be kind? Loving? Patient? Responsible? Fair? Let's think about it.

Determination

"The pessimist sees difficulty in every opportunity.
The optimist sees the opportunity in every difficulty."
- Winston Churchill

For a time, during World War II, little England stood alone in all of Europe against the evil empire that was Nazi Germany. Hitler's forces had swept through Europe like lightening. Country after country fell in rapid succession until the Germans attacked England, and it may have fallen as well had it not been for the dogged determination of its Prime Minister, Winston Churchill. Churchill never considered surrender as an option. He kept England on its feet by the force of his strong will and his optimistic attitude, which refused to accept defeat. Years later, long after the Nazi's had been vanquished, he gave one of his most famous speeches to a class at Harrow School. He rose to the podium, looked out at the crowd with a serious expression and said, "Never give in, never give in, never, never, never, never – in nothing, great or small, large or petty – never give in except to convictions of honor and good sense." Then, he sat down; there was nothing more he needed to say.

This attitude of never giving up is called by many names: perseverance, persistence and determination, to name a few. It is summed up by the old expression "If at first you don't succeed, try, try again." It is more important than talent, intelligence or social status. To coin a new phrase, determination determines success. So, if you are doing well in school, keep up the good work. If your report card was less than you wanted, try again. If your relationship to friends and family is troubled, stay connected to them long enough, and things will get better. In short, never give up.

• • • • • • • • • •

"Nothing in the world can take the place of persistence. Talent will not. Nothing is more common than unsuccessful individuals with talent. Genius will not. Unrewarded genius is almost a proverb. Education will not. The world is full of educated derelicts. Persistence and determination alone are omnipotent."
- Calvin Coolidge

"A man's greatest strength develops at the point where he overcomes his greatest weakness."
- Elmer G. Letterman

"The race is not always to the swift, but to those who keep on running."
- Author Unknown

"Be like a postage stamp – stick to one thing until you get there."
- Margaret Carty

"Opportunity is missed by most people because it is dressed in overalls and looks like work."
- Thomas Edison

You Can't Win
If You're Not in the Game

While leaving a football game, a student from another school was overheard criticizing his team's performance. "If I'd played today, we'd have won," he was saying. Easy to say when you're not on the field. His comment brings to mind Theodore Roosevelt's classic quotation about such criticism:

"It is not the critic who counts, not the man who points out how the strong man stumbles or where the doer of deeds could have done them better. The credit belongs to the man who is actually in the arena, whose face is marred by dust and sweat and blood, who strives valiantly, who errs and comes up short again and again because there is no effort without error and shortcomings, who knows the great devotion, who spends himself in a worthy cause, who at the best knows in the end the high achievement of triumph and who at worst, if he fails while daring greatly, knows his place shall never be with those timid and cold souls who know neither victory nor defeat."

• • • • • • • • • •

"The man who complains about the way the ball
bounces is likely the one who dropped it."
- Lou Holtz

Experience Is the Best Teacher

"Good judgement comes from experience,
and experience comes from bad judgement."
- Barry LePatner

When I read the quotation above, I had to smile. The truth of it has been borne out in my own life many times. Although I have generally tried to be a responsible person, my attempts to make good choices have not always gotten the results I was after. I have learned the hard way, through experience, to choose my friends carefully, to err on the side of caution, to ask questions and do some research before making important decisions and so on. Still, I have occasion to improve my judgement by learning from my mistakes.

This idea was expressed to me first through the expression: "Experience is the best teacher." That's the reason for homework, by the way. People can tell you how to do things or what you should do; but to really understand something, you have to try it yourself.

This does not mean that you have to try everything once. One experience with drugs or alcohol, for example, could ruin your life. As comedian Sam Levenson put it, "You must learn from the mistakes of others; you can't possibly live long enough to make them all yourself."

So, do your best to make responsible choices. Be informed; ask for advice. But remember this, if you are to become the person you were created to be, you must take the risk of making your own choices. The fear of making a mistake has kept many people from reaching their full potential. Timid people tell themselves that they are still making up their minds when, truthfully, they are choosing to let their opportunities pass them by.

T. S. Elliott, the famous poet and essayist, had something to say on this subject. He said, "Only those who will risk going too far can possibly find out how far they can go." And if you learn from your mistakes, you will go far indeed.

• • • • • • • • • •

"Action is character."
- F. Scott Fitzgerald

"Happiness is not the end of life:
character is."
- Henry Ward Beecher

"Courage is being scared to death -
and saddling up anyway."
- John Wayne

"All problems become smaller if you don't
dodge them, but confront them."
- William S. Halsey

"Nurture your mind with great thoughts,
for you will never go any higher than you think."
- Benjamin Disraeli

Doing Your Duty

Eleanor and Franklin Roosevelt are two people that I admire - not just for what they accomplished, but also for what they overcame.   Franklin grew up with the expectation that he would someday follow in the footsteps of his famous relative, Theodore Roosevelt, to become President of the United States. But in mid-life, he was stricken with polio and became paralyzed from the waist down. According to the conventional wisdom of the time, this should have put an end to his political career and dreams of being elected President. Eleanor was a homely child who had the misfortune of being born to one of the most beautiful women of her day. Her mother rejected her because of her looks, referring to her as "Granny." Eleanor's father was an alcoholic who lived in the shadow of his brother, Theodore Roosevelt. He never settled into a career. As bad as this was, things got even worse for Eleanor when both of her parents died and left her an orphan at age nine. From that time until she was grown, she was passed from one relative to another or lived in boarding schools.

But neither Eleanor nor Franklin was willing to accept defeat.   Both of them had been inspired by Theodore Roosevelt's example of meeting every challenge with his fierce determination to succeed, personally, and to do his duty to serve others in his chosen field of politics. For he too had fought against discouragement, having been told as a child that he would never be able to do very much due to his debilitating asthma. Instead of accepting this verdict, he dedicated himself to what he called "the strenuous life," and became known for his physical, as well as mental, prowess.

After years of public service as the wife of President Franklin Delano Roosevelt, Eleanor wrote: "Sometimes you must do the thing you cannot do." In a similar way, we all should refuse to accept a life that is less than the best.

• • • • • • • • •

"To suppose that any form of government will secure liberty or happiness without any virtue in the people is a chimerical idea."
– James Madison

"Good manners are like traffic rules for society."
- Michael Levine

"The first requisite of a good citizen in this Republic of ours is that he shall be able and willing to pull his weight."
- Theodore Roosevelt

"Learn the wisdom of compromise, for it is better to bend a little than to break."
- Jane Wells

"In reading and writing, you cannot lay down rules until you have learnt to obey them. Much more so in life."
- Marcus Aurelius

Better Government

Thomas Jefferson, James Madison and other founders of our country often observed that democracy does not work without a **virtuous** citizenry. Jefferson put it this way: "That government is best which governs least, because its people discipline themselves." In other words, self-government requires self-discipline. To be free, we must voluntarily set limits on ourselves in order to reduce the necessity for laws and law enforcement.

But sometimes, we confuse liberty with a license to do whatever we please regardless of how our actions infringe on the freedom and happiness of others. For example, some talk while the teacher is talking or when their classmates are trying to answer the teacher's questions. In this way, they prevent those who want to learn from learning. Others cut in line in the cafeteria, not caring that they are being unfair to their fellow students. When students behave in this way, teachers and other adults have a duty to discipline them in order to protect the equal rights of all.

So, remember: *If you don't set your own limits, someone else will have to set them for you.*

• • • • • • • • •

"It is the duty of government to make it difficult
for people to do wrong, and easy to do right."
- William Gladstone

Fairness, a Basic American Value

The Declaration of Independence states, "We hold these truths to be self-evident, that all men are created equal, that they are endowed by their Creator with certain unalienable Rights, that among these are Life, Liberty and the pursuit of Happiness." When Thomas Jefferson penned these words, he was clearly expressing what most people think of as the basic belief of our country. But at the time he wrote them, all Americans did not enjoy equal freedom. Most African-Americans were slaves and not one woman had the right to vote. Later in our country's history, Abraham Lincoln wrote that we should do our best to "approximate" (come very close to) the ideal of equal freedom for all even though we may never achieve perfect equality. He freed the slaves, of course, but it was another 55 years before women got the right to vote. Much later, Martin Luther King, Jr. led in the struggle for full civil rights for African-Americans. He, along with thousands of other fair-minded Americans, completed the work that Jefferson, a slaveholder, began. You see, it takes the best efforts of all of us to move our country ever closer to the realization of our dreams.

• • • • • • • • •

"This country will not be a good place
for any of us to live in,
unless it is a good place for all of us to live in."
- Theodore Roosevelt

Freedom is Frightening

On December 7, 1986, *The New York Times Magazine* reported on Russian emigrants who were returning to the Soviet Union voluntarily because they could not handle the freedom in America. Having so many choices and knowing that their fate was in their own hands was too stressful for them. Their experiences here seemed to bear out the beliefs of existentialist philosophers, who have stated that along with death, isolation and meaninglessness, freedom is among the four main causes of anxiety. Why?

Rollo May, philosopher and psychologist, has written that because people know that they are responsible for the choices they make, they often try to escape from freedom, choosing the role of helpless victim or pretending to be powerless in order to avoid responsibility. They say, "it's not my job," "It's the government's fault," "my parents let me down" and otherwise attempt to shift responsibility to others. Unfortunately, when people give away their responsibility in this way, they also give away their freedom and personal power. For them, the opportunity provided by living in the land of the free and the home of the brave is wasted. They may as well live in a totalitarian state.

· · · · · · · · ·

Responsibility is the price of freedom.

Don't Accept Your Label

I once counseled a mother who had labeled her son as "the one who's going to jail." He had been retained the year before and, at mid-year, was in danger of failing again. No one, including myself, had figured out how to motivate him to do his work, and, out of frustration, his own mother had begun to talk about him as if he were hopeless. Tragically, the student accepted his label, and it became a self-fulfilling prophecy.

When relationships between people get to the point of name-calling and labeling, it reflects a failure of caring and fairness. Also, because we are more than "the fat kid," "the clumsy kid," "the lazy kid" or, on the positive side, "the smart one," "the athletic one" or "the beauty," labeling is rather simple-minded. Even so, the more people refer to a person as clumsy, for example, the more self-conscious he becomes and the more he drops things and trips over his own feet. You see, it really takes two people to hang a label on you, the person who labels you and you. As Eleanor Roosevelt put it, "No one can make you feel inferior without your permission."

To avoid labeling others, it helps me to remember that we co-create each other. If I encourage you, I'm helping you to be a better person. If I compare you unfavorably to your brother or sister, I'm leading you to think of yourself as inferior; and that is both unfair and downright mean. The playwright George Bernard Shaw said, "It's easy – terribly easy – to shake a man's faith in himself. To take advantage of that to break a man's spirit is the devil's work." Let's remember that when we are tempted to define other people unfairly, and never let other people define, and thereby, limit you.

• • • • • • • • •

"The ethical duty is to *treat everyone with respect* –
not to respect everyone in the sense that we hold all
people in high esteem or admire them."
— Michael Josephson

"While the people retain their virtue and vigilance,
no administration, by any extreme of wickedness or folly,
can very seriously injure the government
in the short space of four years."
— Abraham Lincoln

"A stumble may prevent a fall."
— English Proverb

"Those who bring sunshine to the lives of others
cannot keep it from themselves."
— Sir James M. Barrie

"If you think about what you ought to do for other people,
your character will take care of itself."
— Woodrow Wilson

"Without civic morality communities perish;
without personal morality their survival has no value."
— Bertrand Russell

First Things First

In a recent column, family psychologist John Rosemond shared the results of a "Survey of Educational Needs" done in 1997 for the South Metro Chamber of Commerce (Dayton, Ohio) Business Advisory Council. He thought it was interesting that what employers looked for first in an employee, before any "marketable" skills, was honesty. After honesty, willingness to cooperate (a sign of respect), ability and willingness to follow directions, positive attitude and punctuality were rated highest. All of these attributes relate to the person's character. Farther down on the list were the math, language arts and computer skills we expect employers to look for first. Why? I think we know why. What good does it do an employer to hire a computer whiz who can't be trusted, one who plays computer games and surfs the web whenever the employer turns her back? If an accountant uses his math skills to embezzle money, no one would want him as an employee, no matter how mathematically skilled he was.

Our first president, George Washington, also ranked honesty as the most desirable character trait. He said, "I hope I shall always possess firmness and virtue enough to maintain what I consider the most enviable of all titles, the character of an 'Honest Man.'" Washington, like Jefferson and Madison, realized that democracy will not work without virtuous citizens; and honesty, it seems to me, is the beginning of virtue. Without honesty among our people, we lose the "social capital" of trust necessary to

any free society.   When we can no longer trust one
another, our democracy will fail.   Let's make sure that
never happens.

• • • • • • • • • •

"Success is getting what you want.
Happiness is liking what you get."
- H. Jackson Brown

"America, at its best, is compassionate...
Where there is suffering, there is duty.
Americans in need are not strangers, they
are citizens; not problems, but priorities;
and all of us are diminished when any are hopeless."

"Americans are generous and strong and decent, not
because we believe in ourselves, but because we hold
beliefs beyond ourselves. When this spirit of citizenship
is missing, no government program can replace it. When
this spirit is present, no wrong can stand against it."
- President George W. Bush
Inaugural Address

"If you don't have enemies, you don't have character."
- Paul Newman

"If a man is to be free, he must be a slave
to those things that make for freedom."
- John F. Kennedy

Learning Is Fun – Really

"Work banishes those three great evils:
boredom, vice, and poverty."
- Voltaire

According to William Glasser, M.D., humans have five real needs. They are survival needs like food, clothing and shelter, a need for love and belonging, a need for some degree of freedom, for personal power and for fun. Interestingly, Dr. Glasser has found that learning is one of our most important means of having fun and helps us get our other needs met as well. I know that sounds crazy to some of you because learning is work. But think about it, most of the things that bring you true happiness are things you are good at. Sports, art and music spring to mind, but what about when you master a difficult math concept or do a really great project? Is there anything more satisfying than that?

If we acknowledge that learning is fun, we may also begin to see that most any task we learn how to do relieves boredom and provides deep satisfaction when well done. Even jobs like cleaning up the kitchen make us proud and happy when we do them well.

Learning useful skills also keeps us out of trouble. The old saying, "Idle hands are the Devil's workshop," still applies. When we attend to our responsibilities like homework and chores, we direct our energy in helpful, rather than harmful, ways.

Finally, learning provides the means of survival for most of us. The things you are learning now are preparing you to make your own way in the world some day.

Enjoy your work.

• • • • • • • • •

"An invasion of armies can be resisted,
but not an idea whose time has come."
                                        - Victor Hugo

"First keep peace within yourself,
then you can also bring peace to others."
                                        - Thomas a Kempis

"For age is opportunity, no less than youth itself,
though in another dress.
And as the evening twilight fades away,
the sky is filled with stars, invisible by the day."
                                        - Henry Wadsworth Longfellow

"Children speak in the field what they hear in the house."
                                        - Scottish Proverb

"When your neighbor's house is on fire,
you put yourself in danger if you don't help extinguish it."
                                        - Chinese Proverb

"If people knew how hard I have had to work
to gain my mastery, it wouldn't seem wonderful at all."
                                        - Michelangelo

Your Personal Best

Athletes sometimes talk about doing their personal best. I like this term. "Personal best" implies that you should judge yourself by how well you are doing with the talents and abilities you were born with. If you play basketball, Michael Jordan may inspire you, but you are not competing with him. You are competing with yourself. Questions like "How much have I improved?" or "What do I need to work on?" are the important ones to ask.

In academics, you are doing your best when you identify your weak areas and work especially hard on them. We have discovered, for example, that the key to improving reading is simply to read at least 20 minutes everyday. Students who have been willing to do this have raised their ranking on standardized reading tests by an average of 16 points. A few years ago, one student raised his score 61 points.

Remember: You never know what you can do until you do your best.

• • • • • • • • • •

"There are no secrets to success. It is the result of preparation, hard work, and learning from failure.
- Gen. Colin Powell

Don't Sell Yourself Short

"Whether you think you can or
think you can't—you're right."
                    - Henry Ford

I used to enjoy reading the comic strip *Pogo*. What I most remember about it is a saying of the title character. After some self-inflicted disaster, he would say, "We have met the enemy, and they is us." I think about this whenever I find myself getting a bad attitude about some situation or some person, and especially, when I catch myself doing what psychologists call "negative self-talk." Negative self-talk is particularly harmful because it is discouragement that comes from inside your own head. Self-defeating messages like, "I'm no good at math" or "I stink at sports" cause us to give up before we begin. Instead of doing our best, learning from our mistakes, and listening to the advice and instruction of those who know how to improve, we tell ourselves that it is just no use to try.

One way that I have learned to counter this kind of thinking is to concentrate on improving my own performance and to stop comparing myself to others. There is always someone else who is better, so beating myself up emotionally for not being the best is a sure way to ruin my day. Doing my personal best, on the other hand, is very satisfying. Even when I do not win the game or solve the equation, I still enjoy myself and improve my skills.

The second defense I have against negative self-talk is the belief that persistence, which is a slow, steady progress toward your goal, is the only way anyone ever achieves anything and that a lack of persistence is the most common reason that the "talented and gifted" fail. After all, successful people do the things that unsuccessful people are not willing to do. It is as simple as that.

Giving up is easy; anyone can do it. To keep going in the face of setbacks and disappointments requires real strength of character and the wisdom to give yourself encouraging, not discouraging, messages.

• • • • • • • • •

"The truth of the matter is that you always know
the right thing to do. The hard part is doing it."
                          - Gen. H. Norman Schwarzkopf

"It is considered broad-minded to say,
'One person's values are as good as another's.'
It is nonsense to say,
'One person's virtues are as good as another's.'"
                          - George Will

"One of the remarkable – if seldom remarked – benefits of
marriage is that it makes kinsmen out of strangers. It
unites kingdoms, settles wars, links cultures and builds
relationships that are all but impossible without marriage."
                          - William Raspberry

T.H.I.N.K.

Sometimes young people show wisdom beyond their years. A friend of mine met such a person last spring. Mark was watching his daughter, Holly, practice with the Spring Valley High School softball team. On the team was an older girl who had earned Holly's respect. After the practice, Mark went over to say "Hello." He noticed that the young lady had writing on her pitching hand. "What is all this?" he asked. She pointed out a couple of scripture verses and shared her thoughts on those. Then Mark asked, "What about this?" and he pointed to the word "THINK." "Oh, that," she said, a bit embarrassed. "You see, I have a problem with my mouth. So, before I speak, I ask myself: Is it True?" She began to point to each letter in turn. "Is it Helpful? Is it Important? Is it Necessary? And is it Kind?"

Mark was impressed with the young athlete's struggle to discipline her mind and speech along with her body, and he shared her story with me. Since much of the trouble in our lives begins with a thoughtless word, he knew I could benefit from it, and so can you. As we go through the day, let's remember to THINK before we speak.

· · · · · · · · · ·

"If money is your hope for independence, you will never have it. The only real security that a man will have in this world is a reserve of knowledge, experience and ability."
                                                    - Henry Ford

What Really Counts?

"Not everything that counts can be counted."
– Albert Einstein

There is a tendency in this age of science and technology to speak of everything, even human beings, only in terms of that which can be measured or observed. Because of this tendency, psychology, which is mainly concerned with things like personality, character and a person's perceptions, is often considered a pseudo or fake science. Psychiatrist Viktor Frankl called this tendency to treat humans as animals to be studied "nothing but" science. He said, "I will agree that human beings are a collection of drives and instincts, but I will never agree that humans are *nothing but* a collection of drives and instincts."

I was reminded of this when report cards came out. One danger of any report that measures a person by a numerical average is that it can be used to judge the person as a whole. However, a report card is not proof that the person with a high average worked hard or that the person with a lower average worked less. That is one reason teacher comments are included on report cards. Statements like "Work improving" or "demonstrates excellent work habits" sometimes appear alongside disappointing grades. As a guidance counselor who starts with students in 6th grade and follows them to the end of middle school, I understand that these comments are a teacher's way of acknowledging that grades do not tell the whole story. I often know how hard it was for a particular student to make a 'C' in a difficult course. I know how much it means for the student who has been trying to make the A-B honor roll for three years to finally make it. It gives me a different perspective. Maybe the numbers lie. Perhaps, when looked at through the lens of character and effort, the student with the best report card is not always the one with the highest average. And perhaps the satisfaction of doing your best and making improvement cannot be measured.

• • • • • • • • •

"Accept the challenges, so that you may know
the exhilaration of victory."
- Gen. George Patton

"Nothing great was ever achieved without enthusiasm."
- Ralph Waldo Emerson

"But neither the wisest constitution nor the wisest laws
will secure the liberty and happiness of a people whose
manners are universally corrupt. He therefore is
the truest friend of the liberty of his country
who tries most to promote its virtue, and who, so far as
his power and influence extend, will not suffer a man to be
chosen into any office of power and trust
who is not a wise and virtuous man."
- John Adams

Unexpected Gifts

When the clock goes off way before daylight, I am not at all pleased. I rise, but I refuse to shine. But after a cup of coffee and a shower, my mind begins to open to the possibilities of the day. I am ready to let good things happen. And that is the way it was this morning. By the time I finally stepped outside, I was receptive to the wonder that awaited me. It was an especially gorgeous sunrise - streaked with iridescent orange, pink and purple hues - and the rays of the sun lit up the fog that was hugging the rolling hills. I felt thankful to be alive and even, to be awake at such an hour.

As I reflected on this experience, I thought about all the times that we are blessed by unexpected gifts. And I wondered how often we miss our blessings because of a stubborn refusal to accept and appreciate certain things. When a gift is not our idea or when it is not exactly what we think we want, we sometimes close our minds and hearts. We reject the offer to be a friend because we want to be the best friend. When uninvited guests surprise us, we groan because the house is a mess. Wishing that we had what others have, we fail to be thankful for what we do have.

Thankfulness is an important trait of all people of character and is one of the secrets of good living. In fact, the greater our appreciation, the happier we are. Therefore, thankfulness is a virtue that maximizes our joys and minimizes our troubles.

Too Soon Old and Too Late Smart

Last year I began to get some particularly unwanted mail at my house - invitations to join the AARP. Apparently, they consider 50 to signal the onset of old age and imminent decrepitude. Personally, I like to think of myself as being in my extremely late forties. At any rate, being 50 has caused me to think about a number of things I should have done earlier in life. Opportunities to further my education, to travel, and to invest some of my income were put off until later. If only I had known then what I know now.

Parents and teachers know what I am talking about. Adults spend a lot of time trying to help students make better decisions than they did. We know that it is a lot easier to get a good education now than it is to try to catch up when you are older and have many responsibilities other than school. And we remember passing by opportunities to learn to play a sport or a musical instrument or to otherwise develop our hidden talents. The following quote by Mark Twain says it well:

"Twenty years from now you will be more disappointed by the things you didn't do than by the ones you did do. So throw off the bowlines. Sail away from the safe harbor. Catch the trade winds in your sails. Explore. Dream. Discover."

· · · · · · · · ·

"The unlived life is not worth examining."
- Author Unknown

Investing Wisely

"Short-term planners always lose.
Long-term planners always win."
- Anonymous

Whether you are investing in the stock market or investing in yourself, it pays to take the long view. Every life, like every stock, has its ups and downs, and it is tempting to sell out or give up when you don't get the results you were after. But if you are working toward a long-term goal, such as raising your final grade or raising your test scores, you know that the work you are doing now will pay off in the end. Daily classwork and homework may not guarantee an 'A' on the next test, but they do ensure that you will succeed eventually.

Every year, our counselors talk to students about goal setting for success. They ask them to examine their academic strengths and weaknesses and to set goals for improvement. For example, a student with a low score in reading comprehension may commit to reading twenty minutes a day and asking himself questions about what he has read. Or a math student may commit to doing all of her homework every day and showing her work so that her teacher can help her learn from her mistakes. In either case, the student is making an investment in his or her own future.

So, think about how you can invest your time and energy every day to reach your dreams. Find the areas that need improvement, set goals, make plans to reach your goals and take immediate action. Then, you will become one of the successful people who do the things that unsuccessful people are *not willing* to do.

• • • • • • • • •

"Think big thoughts, but relish small pleasures."
- H. Jackson Brown, Jr.

"I never feel age...
If you have creative work, you don't have age or time."
- Louise Nevelson

"Experience is the worst teacher; it gives
the test before presenting the lesson."
- Vernon Law

"Most folks are about as happy
as they make up their minds to be."
- Abraham Lincoln

"Goals are dreams with deadlines."
- Author Unknown

"When we see land as a community to which we belong,
we may begin to use it with love and respect."
- Aldo Leopold

"As long as you've got your health, you've got everything."
- Robert A. Baggett, Sr.

The Early Bird and the Late Mouse

One of the funny things about our culture is that we have a number of wise sayings that seem to contradict each other. For every occasion there seems to be both a proverb and a counter-proverb and sometimes it is hard to tell which one is more appropriate. For example, "Absence makes the heart grow fonder" describes how we feel about some of our relationships while "Out of sight, out of mind" is a better characterization for others. "Actions speak louder than words" seems to cancel out "the pen is mightier than the sword," and yet, I believe them equally. "Look before you leap" has kept me out of trouble, but bitter experience has taught me that sometimes "He who hesitates is lost." Dueling proverbs like these point out the need to think deeply about our decisions rather than relying on pat answers that we apply to every situation.

To illustrate this, let us look at a really good one: "The early bird gets the worm." Following this advice generally places us on the path to success. When we get started immediately on work that needs to be done, we usually do a good job and get a good grade. Staying ahead of schedule practically guarantees success and greatly reduces our stress. On the other hand, it is sometimes a mistake to go first. For instance, being the first to jump off of a high place into a lake can mean permanent disability or death. At school, volunteering to present your paper at the first opportunity to "get it over with" can be a mistake if you are not sure you understand the assignment. Therefore, letting someone else go first on some occasions shows wisdom, which brings us to the opposite of the early bird motto: "The second mouse gets the cheese."

• • • • • • • • •

More Dueling Proverbs

"Many hands make light work" or
"Too many cooks spoil the broth."

"Clothes make the man" or
"Don't judge a book by its cover."

"Nothing ventured, nothing gained" or
"Better safe than sorry."

"What will be, will be" or
"Life is what you make it."

"The bigger, the better" or
"The best things come in small packages."

"The more, the merrier" or
"Two's company; three's a crowd."

"What's good for the goose is good for the gander" or
"One man's meat is another man's poison."

From The Good Clean Funnies website, gcfl@gcfl.net

Learn It, Love It, Live It

Thomas Lickona, the author of *Educating for Character,* says that good character develops in three stages: "knowing the good, desiring the good, and doing the good." Therefore, people who want to develop strong characters have to have open minds, open hearts and a willingness to change their habits.

To know the good requires that we think through our beliefs and values, which is hard work. We might have to struggle with issues of right and wrong, to ask the opinions of wise people and to read about those who have triumphed over hardship and obstacles.

Desiring or loving the good requires that we examine our hearts. Are we willing to do what is right even when it may be easier, at least in the short run, to do wrong? What if it means we have to go against our group? After all, Mark Twain had a point when he said, "Be good, and you will be lonely." Having a strong character and being your own person *is* lonely sometimes.

Doing the good requires that we show our character through action. We may have to do what is right when it is not very popular, like being a friend to the student that our friends have decided to pick on because that is the kind thing to do. Or we might have to skip the big game to finish our big project because that is the responsible thing to do.

Building a strong character is not easy, but then nothing worth having ever comes easy. So, take up

the challenge. Learn wisdom, love goodness, and do
what is right.

• • • • • • • • • •

Three Guiding Principles of Good Character

1. Do your best.
2. Do what's right.
3. Treat other people the way you want to
    be treated.

On Parenting

The Democratic Family?

There are three basic types of families: authoritarian, permissive and authoritative. For most of our country's history, American families tended to be authoritarian. This meant that parents were in complete control of the family. Children were "to be seen and not heard." What they thought or felt about parental decisions was of no real importance. But in the 1950s, a change began to take place. Psychologists and others began to say that if America was a democracy, its families should be run democratically. Overtime, this idea took hold, and parents began to give up more and more of their authority to their children. The majority of parents adopted the permissive style of parenting. Where authoritarian parents had been demanding, these permissive parents strove to be emotionally responsive, making few demands on their children. Instead of being bosses to their children, these parents attempted to be their children's friends. Unfortunately, this hands-off style of parenting has not increased our freedom. Rather than raising a nation of democratically-minded citizens, we have produced a record number of bullies who think the rules do not apply to them. Indeed, many Americans today do not understand that democracies even have rules.

The Merriam-Webster Dictionary defines government as "authoritative direction or control." Therefore, those who head democratic governments and families are still obliged to lead the governed and to enforce the rules of society. When parents fail to exercise their legitimate authority, the result is not democracy, but anarchy – no government. Children, not parents, become the tyrants.

Truly democratic parents are authoritative leaders who are both demanding and emotionally responsive. They allow their children to disagree, respectfully, but never to disobey. To help young people internalize values like respect and responsibility, they encourage discussions about family rules and the reasons behind them. In this way, they raise citizens who are *self*-disciplined, *self*-reliant and *self*-confident.

• • • • • • • • • •

"There is a time in the life of every problem when it is big enough to see, yet small enough to solve."
- Mike Leavitt

"Heredity is what sets the parents of a teenager wondering about each other."
- Laurence J. Peter

"In life, all good things come hard, but wisdom is the hardest to come by."
- Lucille Ball

"Insanity is hereditary – you get it from your children."
- Sam Levenson

Good Citizens Are Interdependent

Americans are in love with the myth of the rugged individual. This is the person who can make it on his own and doesn't need anyone else – who goes his own way. I call this a myth because the person who "does his own thing" without any commitment to others is really quite weak and immature. He isolates himself from others because he has not learned how to be around people without losing his individuality. When people disagree with him, he either gets angry and argues or pretends to agree just to have peace. Often, he finds it easier to isolate himself, to be emotionally or physically distant. He thinks he is being independent.

The flip side of this is the overly dependent person. This person is also uncomfortable with disagreement or disapproval. He seeks togetherness and cannot tolerate differences. He likes to say: "We think, we feel, we want." Because he is afraid of being his own person, he has no personal goals. All of his energy goes into relationships, but his neediness is very unattractive.

The mature person knows that real closeness comes from being an individual who is committed to a relationship with other individuals. He accepts the fact that everyone does not always agree with him or approve of him, and he knows how to stay connected with others even when they disagree. He works well with others or on his own. He can depend on others, and others know that they can depend on him. Therefore, he lives a life of interdependence with others, recognizing that life is a mixture of give and take, that we are all in this together, and that we succeed or fail as a team.

• • • • • • • • •

"Equality of respect is the iron-clad logic
of human relations."
 - Alfred Adler

"What is right is right even if no one else is doing it;
what is wrong is wrong even if everyone else is doing it."
 - Author Unknown

"To create one's own world takes courage."
 - Georgia O'Keeffe

"We are not permitted to choose the frame of our destiny.
But what we put into it is ours."
 - Dag Hammarskjold

"We must be the change we wish to see in the world."
 - Ghandi

"A nation, as a society, forms a moral person,
and every member of it is personally responsible
for his society."
 - Thomas Jefferson

"What do I owe to my times, to my country,
to my neighbors, to my friends? Such are the questions
which a virtuous man ought often to ask of himself."
 - Lavater

Cutting the Apron Strings

Mrs. Strong was a scary teacher. On my first day in the 7th grade, she strode back and forth like General Patton haranguing the troops. "This is the year we *cut* your mama's apron strings!" she announced in her gravelly voice. I wasn't exactly sure what that meant, but it sent a chill down my spine. On some level, I probably realized that she was telling us that we were going to be asked to act more grown-up, to be more independent - which was not all bad. Being more independent meant that I would be more free to make my own choices. But what if I made the wrong ones? I would be held responsible for them, and that made me very nervous.

In her unforgettable way, Mrs. Strong had dramatized the crisis of middle school. Like butterflies emerging from their cocoons, students are expected to try their wings and fly on their own for the first time. It is a time of great opportunity and some danger - exciting and scary. The difficulty for parents and teachers lies in deciding how much freedom students can handle and how much sympathy to give them when they are having a tough time. Because adults know that much of our self-esteem is forged by meeting challenges on our own, we try to wean middle school children off of so much "help." If we rescue them too often, we will stunt their emotional growth and they may never be ready for adult life.

Fortunately, most students decide that accepting more responsibility in exchange for more freedom is a good bargain. They may not always act like it, but they are secretly relieved when parents start allowing them to solve their own problems. After all, when Mama cuts the apron strings, she is giving her child a vote of confidence that says, "I know you can do it for yourself."

• • • • • • • • •

"Storms make the oak grow deeper roots."
- George Herbert

"When what we are is what we want to be, that's happiness."
- Malcolm Forbes

"Art, like morality, consists of drawing the line somewhere."
- G. K. Chesterton

"Your goal should be out of reach but not out of sight."
- Anita DeFrantz

"There is no giant step that does it. It's a lot of little steps."
- Peter A. Cohen

"Our greatest glory is not in never failing, but in rising up every time we fail."
- Ralph Waldo Emerson

Determination Makes the Difference

"A determined soul will do more with a rusty
monkey wrench than a loafer will accomplish
with all the tools in a machine shop."
- Rupert Hughes

One of the mistakes many Americans make is to praise people for their talents rather than for their efforts. We sometimes say to young people, "It comes so easy for you. You are so gifted." Not so in Japan. Japanese parents and teachers believe that whatever one's talents, the important question is, "Are you working hard to develop those talents?" If you are not, students who are less gifted will outdo you through determined, consistent effort.

Theodore Roosevelt emphasized this point when he encouraged people to "Do what you can, with what you have, where you are." Rather than complaining about what we don't have, i.e., our lack of ability or resources, Roosevelt suggested that we should focus on our strengths and make the most of them. Often, we can make a lot out of what we think is only a little by simply being determined to succeed.

• • • • • • • • • •

"I know God will not give me anything I cannot handle.
I just wish he didn't trust me so much."
- Mother Teresa

The Times Are A-Changin' Again

In the 1960s, we sang a lot about freedom and looked forward to a day when we would all be totally free. As we learn to cope with the challenges of this new millennium, however, it is beginning to dawn on us that total freedom for even one person is an impractical idea. Because each person's freedom eventually brings him into conflict with others who want to exercise their own fair share of freedom, mature people are coming to understand that rules and limits are cool after-all. While "No Limits" may still have appeal as an advertising slogan, it is a sure path to disaster as a life-style choice. People who try to live without rules of behavior become bullies and soon ruin all of their relationships. So, unless you want to live alone on a desert island, you would be wise to set reasonable limits on your freedom.

• • • • • • • • •

"You only live once, but if you work it right,
once is enough."
- Joe E. Lewis

"Kind words can be short and easy to speak,
but their echoes are truly endless."
- Mother Teresa

Horse Sense for Parents

"Pet him like you like him."
- Anonymous Horse Trainer

Since moving to the country a few years ago, I've been able to live out some of my youthful cowboy fantasies as the owner of two quarter horses. In the process, I've found that horses are a lot like children. You get much further with kind, firm discipline than you do with strong-arm tactics.

I learned my first lesson from Ranger. Ranger, AKA Bruiser, jumped out from under me the first day I took him out for a ride. I had fallen, literally, for the belief that the best way to show him who was boss was to force him to do something he did not want to do. When the stiffness went away, I began to reconsider my tough-guy approach with this somewhat "spooky" mount.

The most persistent problem I had with Ranger was getting him to take the bridle bit into his mouth. He would clamp his jaws like a kid refusing to take bad-tasting medicine. For months I used the tried and true method of sticking my thumb in the gap between his front teeth and his molars. In this way, I could eventually force the bit in, but it was an unpleasant procedure. Once, he accidentally bit me during this ordeal, and neither one of us liked it very much.

To break the battle of wills, I began to place the bit in the palm of my hand on top of a pile of sweet feed, and

Ranger would gobble it up, bit and all. Then I would pet him and say, "That's a good boy."

After a few weeks of this, I started changing the order of things. I'd put the bit in his mouth and then, reward him with the feed and more petting and praising. Sometimes, he would revert to his old ways, and I would have to force the bit in before I could reward him. On those days, I followed the old horse trainer's adage, "Pet him like you like him," even though I felt like smacking him on the neck.

In this way, I gained his trust and convinced him that I did not want to hurt him. Now he takes the bit better than most and seldom argues with me about anything. He goes where I ask, at the speed I want, and I tell him he's a good boy.

• • • • • • • • •

"All the love we come to know in life springs
from the love we knew as children."
- Marcellus

"If you're ridin', you're trainin'."
- Rick Baggett, a real cowboy

"All happy people are grateful. Ungrateful people
cannot be truly happy. We tend to think that
being unhappy leads people to complain, but
it's truer to say that complaining leads
to people becoming unhappy.
- Dennis Prager

Meaningful Meals

According to Realage.com, a website sponsored by Oprah Winfrey, eating meals together as a family can be good for your emotional health. The site reports that "a recent study revealed that adolescents who frequently ate meals with family members were less likely to need mental health counseling compared to youths who rarely ate with family members." Why? I would guess that eating together is a natural way to strengthen family bonds. When parents make family meals a priority, they send a clear message that they care about their children and want to spend time with them. After all, it can be a lot of trouble to have an "organized supper," as my children call it. And you do have to turn off the TV to do it right, which is unheard of in some households.

Family therapists have long encouraged parents to eat with their children on a regular basis and to develop and maintain other family rituals. Shared meals, birthdays, anniversaries, religious holidays and other special occasions are ways to take a stand for your own family values. These occasions give children a clear sense of what it means to be a part of your particular family and helps them to develop their own identities as individuals who truly belong.

• • • • • • • • •

"It's not that nice guys finish last.
Nice guys are winners before the game even starts."
- Addison Walker

Everyday Heroes

Legendary child psychiatrist Bruno Bettelheim once said that young people don't ask themselves "Do I want to be good?" but rather "Whom do I want to be like?" When I think back to my own childhood and middle school years, my memories are filled with a wide variety of heroes, some better than others. I grew up with Roy Rogers, Fess Parker as Davy Crockett, Elvis, Robin Hood, Tarzan, and later, the Beatles. Even more influential were the adults in my life: my parents, my teachers at school and church, ministers, relatives, neighbors and youth leaders. They were the real heroes who shaped my life.

CHARACTER COUNTS! promotes a T.E.A.M. approach to character education. Adults are to **teach** good ethical values, to **enforce** limits and high expectations, to **advocate** good character (be enthusiastic) and to **model** good character. Heroes and role models do all of these things, and none of them can be left out. But we need to remember that while children may not always do as we say, they will never fail to follow our example. Never forget that you are a hero to some child, yours and possibly, many others.

● ● ● ● ● ● ● ● ●

"I think the one lesson I have learned is that there is no substitute for paying attention."
- Diane Sawyer

"There's no such thing as somebody else's child."
- Bill Russell

Say Something Nice

At certain stages of life, children teach us the difference between loving someone and liking them. When each of my children was six years old, my wife turned to me at some point and said, "He/she has a character disorder. It must be genetic. I know we're not that bad as parents." I found this quite upsetting coming from a pediatrician. But after she had time to calm down and think, Teresa would remember to consult *Your six-year-old: loving and defiant* by Louise Ames. This wonderful book – part of a series on children at various ages and stages – described our children so well that I half-expected to see their pictures in there. Everything they were doing was a normal part of being six. But knowing that defiance and generally obnoxious behavior is what six-year-olds do did not solve the problem. Our relationships with our young children continued to be strained.

Luckily, a friend with an older and much more difficult child had already found the key to healing a bruised and battered relationship. Some very wise person had told her to say one nice thing about her child each night as she tucked him into bed. Just one thing that she liked about him was enough. And like magic, her relationship with her son began to turn around. I suspect this works on middle schoolers and adults as well.

There's No Place Like Work

*"We have to love those who are nearest to us in our own family.
Love will then go out to all who need us."*
                                        – Mother Teresa

I borrowed the title of this essay from a book by Brian C. Robertson. The central idea of the book is that the most significant cultural change of the last thirty years has been in the way we divide our time between work and family. Increasingly, work takes more and more of our time and children get what is left over – what we call "quality time." Citing some pretty grim research findings on increases in self-destructive and violent behavior by young people, the author argues persuasively that Americans need to find a better balance between work and family. Children need more adult supervision than they are getting and parents have a responsibility to see that they get it.

Robertson maintains that this shuffling of priorities reflects a shift in American values. At every other time in American history, most adults worked to provide for the needs of the family. We believed that if the family was doing well and our children were growing up to be good citizens, then we were successful individuals. Today, he says, we work for an entirely different reason: to achieve self-fulfillment through our career. Meeting the needs of our own family is seen as a small thing compared to what we can accomplish at work. Ironically, this attitude is so pervasive that even some of us who work in helping professions are tempted to be more concerned about meeting the needs of CHILDREN than the needs of our own child. After all, nobody gets his or her name in the newspaper for being a *good* parent. And spending time with our children does not fill our pockets with cash. However, it does help us discover the meaning and connection that so many are busily pursuing, but not finding, at work.

• • • • • • • • •

"At work, any of us can be replaced;
at home, none of us can."
- R. B.

"Children have more need of models than of critics."
- Carolyn Coats

"He has the right to criticize
who has the heart to help."
- Abraham Lincoln

"Parents wonder why the streams are bitter,
when they themselves have poisoned the fountains."
- John Locke

"Everybody gets so much information all day long
that they lose their common sense."
- Gertrude Stein

Say What You Mean, Mean What You Say

Integrity is an important part of trustworthiness. A person with integrity says what he means and means what he says. The following story is about a parent who knew how to discipline with love and integrity.

A certain man became angry with his son for his disobedience. In his anger, the father told his son: "You will spend all day Saturday in the room over the garage." Now, this was a room without a television, a telephone or even a radio. All it had in it was a couple of old comfortable chairs and a shelf full of books. The punishment was fair, considering what the boy had done; yet, his father began to worry that a day of complete isolation might not be good for the boy. He wanted to change the punishment, but he had learned long ago never to make idle threats if he wanted his children's respect. After careful consideration, he came up with a way to be true to his word while letting his son know that he cared. The boy still had to spend the day in the boring old room. However, he did it with his father for company.

• • • • • • • • • •

"We make a living by what we get;
we make a life by what we give."
- W. A. Nance

Life Is Not Fair

Occasionally, someone will observe that life is not fair. It is another one of those self-evident truths. We find that sometimes cheaters do prosper, for a time at least, and that bad things happen to good people. Still, we don't want to accept unfairness, and it is necessary for someone to state the obvious once in a while. Unfairness is unavoidable, and it is important for our mental health that we accept this fact. On the other hand, if we are to be people of character, we must make sure that we are not the instruments of unnecessary or avoidable unfairness. If we are playing or coaching a game, we can't stop the baseball from taking a funny bounce and causing a good player to miss a catch, but we can make sure that the rules of the game are followed to the best of our ability. This takes maturity and judgement, which comes only through experience.

Parents have a special duty to model fairness. The Josephson Institute of Ethics offers the following "Parent's Pledge" as a guideline:

> I will not resort to arbitrary power to get my way when I have taught that general rules of fairness are applicable.
> I will treat all my children, including stepchildren, equally and fairly.
> I will be open and reasonable to discussion and criticism.

The last item is particularly difficult for most parents because it asks us to maintain our authority as adults and show respect for the thoughts and feelings of children at the same time. Ironically, our authority gains validity with children when they can see that we are fair and that we respect their feelings.

• • • • • • • • •

"The important thing is this: To be able at any moment to sacrifice what we are for what we could become."
- Charles du Bois

"You are the bows from which your children as living arrows are sent forth."
- Kahlil Gilbran

"The value of marriage is not that adults produce children but that children produce adults."
- Peter de Vries

"We aim above the mark to hit the mark."
- Ralph Waldo Emerson

"If you lead through fear you will have little to respect; but if you lead through respect, you will have little to fear."
- Author Unknown

"This thing we call failure is not the falling down, but the staying down."
- Mary Pickford

Make Your Life Easier

Accepting your limits is essential to the proper exercise of freedom, and it makes life so much easier. Many of life's difficult problems and temptations become no-brainers when you simply decide in advance that some things are not a choice. Then, you don't even have to think about it. Drugs? Off limits! Premarital sex? Not one of my choices. Is homework optional? I don't think so. Acting like what I have to say is so important that I can dominate the class discussion? Disrespectful; not who I am. Of course, you have to do a lot of thinking about what is really important before most of your questions are settled, but accepting that some things are off limits is a step in the right direction.

• • • • • • • • • •

"Enjoy the little things, for one day you may look back and realize they were the big things."
– Robert Brault

"The long fight to save wild beauty represents democracy at its best. It requires citizens to practice the hardest of virtues – self-restraint."
- Edwin Way Teale

"One must learn by doing the thing, for though you think you know it, you have no certainty until you try."
- Aristotle

Find Your Place through Usefulness

Alfred Adler, the great child-rearing expert, said that we find our place through usefulness. My wife had her own way of saying this whenever our young children misbehaved. She would say, "They don't have enough to do." Then, she or I would find some useful task for them to perform. We never gave them busy work; always, it was something that needed to be done. Surprisingly, after only a few minutes of working on their assignment, the children would be quite happy and ready to use their creativity in more constructive ways. This parental intervention never failed. Why? I think it worked because the job would give the children a sense of their value to the family. They understood that the service they performed was truly appreciated.

Contrast this with another approach to life that is becoming increasingly common. This could be summed up as "find your place through uselessness." In this scheme, a person tries to make the case that he is a victim, is helpless, maybe even pitiful. His position in society is the one who needs to be taken care of. His bad behavior needs to be understood and tolerated. He can't be held responsible for doing his own work, let alone doing anything for the good of the family or group. It is a depressing way to get through life, but many see it as an easy road.

Let's try to remember that the easy way always turns out to be the hardest way in the end. Also, if we really want to find our place, we must do it through usefulness.

Up Close and Personal

When I think about the holidays, I think about not only the fun, but also, the stress of spending lots and lots of time with family. Sometimes the expectations for the "perfect" holiday set us up for disappointment in the real world where individual differences guarantee that we will have a few disagreements. These disagreements don't have to be unpleasant, however. The following story illustrates how respect and impeccable manners can prevent differences from driving a wedge between you and the people you love.

One summer, my friend John went on a road trip with his wife, his son and his mother-in-law. John was really enjoying a country rock CD by an artist named Lucinda Williams. He played it again and again ....and again. After about 150 miles of this music, his mother-in-law asked in a pleasant voice, "John, do you have any other music that is as good as this?"

In a polite way that acknowledged John's right to his own musical tastes, she let him know that she was ready for something different. What a great example of disagreeing without being disagreeable.

• • • • • • • • •

"When you blame others, you give up
your power to change."
- Douglas Noel Adams

Real Self-esteem

Are parents today killing their children with kindness? That is the contention of John Rosemond, the syndicated columnist and parenting expert. Dr. Rosemond, a psychologist, says that parents have been led to believe that how a child feels about himself from moment to moment is more important than the behaviors and habits that lead to the formation of good character and long-term success. "Grandma was concerned with character and behavior," he says. "Today's parents focus on personality development and feelings." He believes that this focus on feelings causes us to pamper children out of worry over their self-esteem, but that, ironically, pampering prevents children from developing the good work habits and character traits that build real self-esteem.

It is only when we demand perfection from children, rather than their best efforts, that we begin to damage their self-esteem. Expressing a firm belief in a student's ability to succeed and refusing to listen to excuses is not harmful and is, in fact, an affirmation of his or her intrinsic worth. This stance meets the real emotional need of children to feel competent and leads to the development of a positive self-image and true self-esteem.

• • • • • • • • • •

"The reason grandparents and grandchildren get along
so well is that they have a common enemy."

- Sam Levenson

Character Matters Most

"I have a dream my four little children will one day live in a nation where they will not be judged by the color of their skin but by the content of their character."
- Martin Luther King, Jr.

Whenever we observe Martin Luther King's birthday, I think of his "I have a dream" speech and about the progress we have made toward his clearly stated goal: that we will judge people by the character they show rather than by their skin color.

Growing up in the South, I lived in a segregated society, and I went to segregated public schools until my senior year in high school. So, I have seen much progress in this area, but there is still plenty of work to be done in the area of respect for people of other races and cultures.

A bigger issue is the matter of judging people by their character more than by any other measure. Many social commentators point out that Americans are more likely to judge one another by the content of their bank accounts than by the content of their characters. Dr. James Fowler of Harvard University, believes that the primary values of most Americans are the values of consumerism. These values tell us "that you should experience everything you desire, own everything that you want and relate intimately with whomever you wish." Whether we agree with these values or not, they are the values that are advertised, literally, in our culture. Parents and teachers need to take an active role in emphasizing character values if we hope to counteract these toxic messages.

As I go around the classrooms, I see that teachers do believe that character is the true measure of success. Banners on the walls say things like "Your I will is more important than your IQ," or "Your attitude is more important than your ability." These banners hint at the truth: compared with talent, ability, money, race, gender or social status, character matters most.   Let us make sure all of our children understand this vital truth.

• • • • • • • • • •

"Nothing about character is hereditary. Everyone,
regardless of social background, financial status, race,
or sex, enters the world with an equal opportunity
to become a person of great or petty character."
- Michael Josephson

"There is more to life than increasing its speed."
- Mohandas K. Gandhi

"We can't become what we need to be
by remaining what we are."
- Oprah Winfrey

"A wise man will make more opportunities than he finds."
- Francis Bacon

"All receive advice. Only the wise profit from it."
- Syrus

Bibliography

Barnette, Henlee H. *Introducing Christian Ethics.* Nashville: Broadman Press, 1961.

Berry, Wendell. *Sex, Economy, Freedom & Community.* New York: Pantheon Books, 1993.

Bowen, Murray. *Family Therapy in Clinical Practice.* Northvale, New Jersey: Jason Aronson, 1985.

Corsini, Raymond J. and Danny Wedding, eds. *Current Psychotherapies.* Itasca, Illinois: F. E. Peacock Publishers, Inc., 1989.

Dreikurs, Rudolf and Vicki Soltz. *Children: The Challenge.* New York: A Plume Book, 1987.

Fisher, Helen E. *Anatomy of Love: a Natural History of Mating, Marriage and Why We Stray.* New York: Fawcett Columbine, 1994.

Frankl, Viktor E. *Man's Search for Meaning.* New York: Simon & Schuster, 1984.

Fukuyama, Francis. *The Great Disruption: Human Nature and the Reconstitution of Social Order.* New York: The Free Press, 1999.

Fukuyama, Francis. *Trust: The Social Virtues and the Creation of Prosperity.* New York: Touchstone Books, 1996.

Gilbert, Roberta M. *Extraordinary Relationships: A New Way of Thinking About Human Interactions.* Minneapolis, MN: CHRONIMED Publishing, 1992.

Harrison, Lawrence E. *The Pan-American Dream: Do Latin America's Cultural Values Discourage True Parnership with the United States and Canada?* New York: Basic Books, 1997.

Jastrow, Robert. *God and the Astronomers.* New York: W. W. Norton & Company, 1978.

Kerr, Michael E. and Murray Bowen. *Family Evaluation.* New York: W. W. Norton & Company, 1988.

King, Martin Luther, Jr. *I Have a Dream: Writings and Speeches that Changed the World.* New York: HarperCollins, 1992.

Kilpatrick, William. *Why Johnny Can't Tell Right from Wrong: Moral Illiteracy and the Case for Character Education.* New York: Simon & Schuster, 1992.

Lewis, C. S. *The Four Loves.* London: Fount, 1998.

Lewy, Guenter. *Why America Needs Religion: Secular Modernity and Its Discontents.* Grand Rapids, Michigan/Cambridge, U. K.: Wm. B. Eerdmans Publishing Company, 1996.

Lickona, Thomas. *Educating for Character: How our Schools Can Teach Respect and Responsibility.* New York: Bantam Books, 1991.

Oates, Wayne E. *The Struggle to Be Free: My Story and Your Story.* Philadelphia: The Westminster Press, 1983.

Peck, M. Scott. *People of the Lie: The Hope for Healing Human Evil.* New York: Simon & Schuster, 1983.

Peck, M. Scott. *The Road Less Traveled: A New Psychology of Love, Traditional Values and Spiritual Growth.* New York: A Touchstone Book, 1978.

Remboldt, Carole and Richard Zimman. *Respect & Protect.* Minneapolis: Johnson Institute, 1996.

Robertson, Brian C. *There's No Place Like Work: How Business, Government, and Our Obsession with Work Have Driven Parents from Home.* Dallas, Texas: Spence Publishing Co., 2000.

Rosemond, John. *A Family of Value.* Kansas City, Missouri: Andrews and McMeel, 1995.

Sayers, Dorothy Leigh and Mary M. Shideler (illustrator). *Are Women Human?* Grand Rapids: Wm. B. Eerdmans Publishing Company, 1986.

Wills, Garry. *Lincoln at Gettysburg: The Words that Remade America.* New York: A Touchstone Book, 1992.

Wilmes, David J. *Parenting for Prevention.* Minneapolis: Johnson Institute, 1995.

Wilson, James Q. *The Marriage Problem: How Our Culture Has Weakened Families.* New York: HarperCollins, 2002.

Video Sources

Let's Teach Character, VHS, 1996. Marina del Rey, California: Josephson Institute of Ethics.

Making Ethical Decisions, VHS, 1994-1997. Marina del Rey, California: Josephson Institute of Ethics.

Index